ST. THOMAS AQUINAS

ON SPIRITUAL
CREATURES

(De Spiritualibus Creaturis)

MEDIAEVAL PHILOSOPHICAL TEXTS

IN TRANSLATION NO. 5

3+4

ST. THOMAS AQUINAS

ON SPIRITUAL CREATURES

(De Spiritualibus Creaturis)

Translated from the Latin
with an introduction

by

Mary C. FitzPatrick, Ph.D.

in collaboration with

John J. Wellmuth, Ph.D.

MARQUETTE UNIVERSITY PRESS   MILWAUKEE, WISCONSIN

Nihil Obstat

Gerard Smith, S.J., censor deputatus
Milwaukiae, die 25 mensis Martii, 1949

Imprimi Potest

Leo D. Sullivan, S.J., Praep. Provinc. Prov.
Chicagiensis, die 28 mensis Martii, 1949

Imprimatur

✝Moyses E. Kiley
Archiepiscopus Milwaukiensis
Milwaukiae, die 5 mensis Aprilis, 1949

Second Printing 1969
Third Printing 1981

ISBN-087462-205-0

Printed in the United States of America

CONTENTS

PREFATORY REMARKS

THIS translation was originally undertaken at the request of Mother Margaret Reilly, R.S.C.J., president of Barat College of the Sacred Heart in Lake Forest, Illinois. Its completion is due in great part to her kind encouragement but most of all to the unfailing and unstinted work of my collaborator, Father John J. Wellmuth, S.J., formerly chairman of the Department of Philosophy at Loyola University in Chicago and now filling a like post at Xavier University in Cincinnati. To him I am greatly indebted for numerous elucidations of the thought of St. Thomas, much helpful criticism, and innumerable suggestions for more felicitous turns of phrase. During the time of our work together the entire manuscript was revised and every effort was made to keep the style of the translation as close to that of the original as the exigencies of the English language permit.

The translation has been made from the critical text of Father Leo Keeler.[1] That editor's notes have also been incorporated. The arrangement of these has been faithfully preserved, including the references at the beginning of the notes on each Article to other works of St. Thomas as well as to those of other Christian writers and ancient or mediaeval philosophers where the same problems as are handled in the Articles are also discussed. All other references, after being carefully checked and corrected occasionally where typographical errors had occurred in the Keeler text, have been left within brackets in the body of the translation. English words within parentheses owe their presence to the parentheses used in Father Keeler's text. Wherever Latin words occur in the body of the translation, they have been taken from the Latin text to clarify the translation where that seemed advisable.

---

[1] *Sancti Thomae Aquinatis Tractatus De Spiritualibus Creaturis* (Rome, 1937).

[1]

ST. THOMAS AQUINAS
ON SPIRITUAL CREATURES

TRANSLATOR'S INTRODUCTION

I. The Mediaeval Disputation

Since *De Spiritualibus Creaturis* belongs to that form to which the Scholastic philosophers applied the name disputation, it would seem well to examine in some detail the origin, the nature and the use of the disputation as a teaching device in the mediaeval universities.

During the Middle Ages methods of teaching were largely conditioned by a paucity of texts, for printing was as yet unknown and the only available books were in the form of manuscripts that had been laboriously copied by hand. These could only be obtained with the greatest difficulty either through purchase or rental. Consequently the master was forced to read *(legere)*[2] those texts he wanted his students to know. During the course of such reading not all the thoughts or the implications of the passage were clearly understood. In order that he might insure his pupil's having a firm grasp of the thought, the master frequently made explanations of difficult passages either by a paraphrase or by still further exposition of the thought. At times the passage that was being read might raise a problem in a student's mind. In that case the student was led to ask questions or, failing that, the master himself might raise the issue that he wanted discussed, guide the pupil toward the desired solution or, if a pupil utterly failed to grasp the point, himself give the explanation or proof. As students advanced in knowledge and attainments, a capable master would often pose questions on dogmatic or moral theology, canon law, or liturgy. These could take the simplest form, that of question and answer, or the form of question that was known as a disputation *(disputatio ordinaria; quaestio disputata)*.

By the thirteenth century the disputation had been entirely separated from the interpretation of any text and was a separate and public part of the master's lesson. The question or the thesis to be disputed was set in advance by the master who was to conduct the disputation. It, together with its date, was announced in the other schools of the faculty in order that the other faculty and student members of the university might attend. Usually the subjects chosen by each master varied, because ordinarily

---

[2] Hence the derivation of our English word "lecture" and the German *vorlesung* as a teaching device.

each professor held but a small number of disputations annually. When, as St. Thomas did, a master held disputations every two weeks or even weekly, he could take a central theme as, for instance, *De Spiritualibus Creaturis,* which would form the material for a more or less long series of disputations. His *Disputed Questions* vary in length from the five that comprise *De Unione Verbi Incarnati* to the one hundred twenty-four that compose *De Veritate.*

On the day of a disputation all lessons given by the other masters and bachelors of the faculty stopped. Only the master who was giving the disputation on that day had a short lesson for his students before the others arrived. Once the visitors were assembled, the disputation began. It was held under the master's direction although he himself did not directly dispute. His bachelor took on the role of respondent or defender of the thesis, thus beginning his apprenticeship in such exercises. Objections to the thesis were presented by the other masters and bachelors who were present and, if there were time, by students. The bachelor answered the arguments and, if necessary, the master came to his assistance, although the bachelor was meant to bear the brunt of sustaining the argument. The objections were not raised according to any order that had been established beforehand. When all objections were in and answered, the actual disputation was at an end.

Notes on the proceedings were kept which, however, at the end of the disputation still presented but a disordered and chaotic mass of material. In order to give it a logical form the master worked over the arguments pro and con, reducing them to a definite form; then he "determined" the truth of the matter; that is, gave a definite form to the views on the subject that he proposed henceforth to hold. Only a master had the right to "determine" a question.

The determination took place at the first meeting of the class after the actual disputation. First, the material was coordinated as far as possible in logical order by presenting all the objections that had been advanced against the thesis. These were followed by the arguments in favor of the thesis. From that point he passed on to a further exposition of the question, the answer *(responsio),* which formed the central and essential part of the determination, wherein he definitely formulated his own views on the question. This in turn was succeeded by an individual answer to each objection that had been advanced against the thesis. If there was any opportunity to do so, this in turn was followed by supplementary information. Once "determined", the matter of the disputation was committed to writing by the master.

St. Thomas conducted hundreds of such disputations, which collectively form his *Quaestiones Disputatae.* Among them are to be found his disputations *De Veritate, De Potentia, De Malo, De Unione Verbi Incarnati, De Spiritualibus Creaturis, De Anima* and *De Virtutibus*.

II. The Structural Form of a *Disputed Question*

De Spiritualibus Creaturis belongs to that group of St. Thomas' works which is known as *Quaestiones Disputatae* or *Disputed Questions*. While all share a common form, the following remarks apply specifically to the series of *Disputed Questions* that deals with spiritual creatures.

This series breaks down the broad general topic "spiritual creatures" into eleven subdivisions, each of which handles one particular aspect of the subject. These are known as "articles." Each begins with the posing of a question about spiritual creatures; for instance, Article I puts the following question: "Is spiritual substance composed of matter and form?" An affirmative answer follows immediately in this Article, although this is not the case with regard to all the articles. The answer in Article II, for example, is made in the negative. Objections to the thesis are then brought forward. These are based on statements that are taken from the Bible, the works of the Church Fathers, or the writings of pagan and Christian philosophers. Aristotle is frequently cited, invariably under the name of "the Philosopher." Averroes, the Arabian commentator on the works of Aristotle, is also often referred to, but almost always as "the Commentator." In Article I twenty-five such objections are raised. These in turn are followed by fourteen arguments in support of the thesis.

The most significant part of an article is, however, the "answer", where St. Thomas resolves the objections to the thesis and, by stating his own views on the matter, gives a definitive form to the doctrine that he holds and proposes to teach. The last part of the answer is always devoted to a point by point rebuttal of each of the objections that have been made against the thesis. As in the case of the objections, views are supported by quotations from ecclesiastical and philosophical writings, so also in the rebuttal recourse is had to the same sort of writings.

III. Date and Place of Composition of *De Spiritualibus Creaturis*

The question of the date and place of composition of *De Spiritualibus Creaturis* confronts the investigator with many difficulties. The problem is an important one, for by its ultimate solution differing data concerning St. Thomas' life and the development of his thought can be fixed. During the first three decades of this present century a healthy controversy raged on the point, yet even now the matter in all its aspects has by no means been conclusively settled, the evidence thus far assembled being subject to more or less subjective interpretation.

The arguments whereby the chief figures in the controversy support their various positions are based on 1) old catalogues of the works of St. Thomas, 2) apparent interrelations between *De Spiritualibus Creaturis* and others of the *Quaestiones Disputatae,* 3) various bits of internal evidence within the work itself.

The data to be gathered from the catalogues is highly unsatisfactory.[3] The official catalogue of the proceedings of St. Thomas' canonization divides the *Quaestiones Disputatae* into three groups: 1) those written in Paris (1256-1259); 2) those composed in Italy (1260-1268); 3) those written in Paris during the Saint's second stay there (1268-1272). Only one work is mentioned by name for each period, this name being followed by the cryptic phrase *et ultra.* Consequently there is no definite information about *De Spiritualibus Creaturis* to be gleaned from this source. As for the catalogue compiled by Ptolemy of Lucca, Ptolemy definitely places the work as having been written in Italy in the time of Pope Clement IV (1265-1268). Unfortunately this information is not conclusive, as Ptolemy is notorious for the unreliability of his information. Other catalogues, such as those of Bernardo Guido, Pierre Roget, Louis of Valladolid, St. Antoninus, John of Colonna, and the *Tabula Scriptorum Ordinis Praedicatorum* include our work by name but furnish no further information, while that of William of Tocco omits any mention of it. Accordingly the catalogues are of little or no help. Nor in the lists of St. Thomas' works that were circulated by the booksellers of Paris[4] during the thirteenth and fourteenth centuries do we find much to aid us. They mention our work, but follow no fixed order nor do they make any attempt to indicate its date or its place of composition.

Nor does the second type of evidence supply any more definite information. In several articles of *De Spiritualibus Creaturis* St. Thomas sets forth his teaching on the soul, a subject that is discussed more fully in *De Anima.* This circumstance caused Father Madonnet to assert[5] that our work was composed prior to *De Anima* and to note what he termed a particularly close correspondence between portions of the two.[6] In this regard, however, Father Keeler[7] remarks that there is no explicit reference in either work to the other. In the place already cited Father Mandonnet also maintains that Siger of Brabant consulted *De Spiritualibus Creaturis* before writing his *De Anima Intellectiva* (q. 7, *ad fin.*) in 1271, but, as Father Keeler again notes, the information on which this statement is made is not entirely certain.

---

[3] Cf. P. Mandonnet (*Revue Thomiste* XXIII (1918) pp. 277-278), where the evidence of the catalogues is assembled.
[4] *Chartularium Univ. Paris.* I, p. 646; II, p. 108.
[5] *Bulletin Thomiste* (1924) p. 59.
[6] Cf. *De An.* VI, ad 13 with *De Sp. Cr.* II, VIII; *De An.* VII with *De Sp. Cr.* I, II, III, V; *De An.* VIII with *De Sp. ,Cr.* II; *De An.* IX with *De Sp. Cr.* I; *De An.* XIX with *De Sp. Cr.* XI.
[7] *De Sp. Cr.,* ed. critica (Rome, 1937) pp. xi-xii.

Father Glorieux used the aforesaid similarity between our work and *De Anima* to build up his theory that *De Spiritualibus Creaturis* had been composed at Viterbo in Italy.[8] In his view St. Thomas, not having time to edit this series of questions before leaving Italy, brought them along to Paris with him where, after working them over again, he used them in his battle with the Averroists. This same evidence Father Pelster[9] likewise uses in support of an Italian origin for *De Spiritualibus Creaturis*. According to his theory the Angelic Doctor, having written *Summa contra Gentiles,* which deals with Averroism, while he was in Italy, there is no improbability in his having written our work, which in part touches on some of the same themes, at the same time. These various theories are extremely ingenious, but can scarcely be classed as definitive evidence. Nor can we place much trust in the arithmetical computations of Mandonnet,[10] whereby he sought to prove the number of disputations that were held by St. Thomas in given years and thereby establish the dates and places of composition of the various *Quaestiones Disputatae,* since these computations are much too subjective and uncertain to be given much credence.

With regard to internal evidence, much has been made of the passage in Article IX (ad 11), apparently first noted by Georg von Hertling[11] in 1881, where the river Seine[12] is referred to in this fashion: "as the Seine river is not 'this' particular river because of 'this' flowing water, but because of 'this' source and 'this' bed etc." From it von Hertling made the deduction that the example of the Seine would be appropriate only if the question had been disputed at Paris. Many years later Mandonnet[13] also became a fervent champion of this view and has heatedly defended it against all adversaries. Others, seeking to combat this thesis, have brought to light several variant readings in the manuscripts. At least fifteen different manuscripts were examined ranging in date from the thirteenth to the fifteenth centuries. One of these[14] yielded the reading *fluvius Renus,* which has been taken to refer to the German Rhine on the banks of which St. Thomas studied under Albertus

---

[8] P. Glorieux, "Les Questions disputées de S. Th. et leur suite chronologique." *Recherches de théol. anc. et médiévale* IV (1932) pp. 19-20.
[9] F. Pelster, "Zur Datierung der Quaestio disputata de Sp. Cr." *Gregorianum* VI (1925) p. 237.
[10] P. Mandonnet. "Chronologie des Questions disputées de S. Th. d' Aquin." *Revue Thomiste* XXIII (1918) pp. 341-371.
[11] "Wo und wann verfasste Th. von Aquin die Schrift de Sp. Cr.?" *Hist. Jahrb.* V (1884) p. 145; cf. J. A. Endres in *G. von Hertling: Historisches Beiträge* (München, 1914) pp. 16-19.
[12] P. Synave makes a telling point when he insists that the demonstratives *hic, hanc, hunc* in the Latin of this passage would not have been used had the Seine not been a nearby river (*Bulletin Thomiste* I, p. 2).
[13] *Op. cit.,* pp. 284 ff.
[14] Cod. Balliolensis 47 (of the 13th or 14th century).

Magnus. Father Pelster,[15] however, believes that not the Rhine is meant but rather the little river Renus in Italy which flows past Bologna, making this reading serve to bolster his thesis that *De Spiritualibus Creaturis* was written in Italy. Another manuscript[16] supplies *fluvius Corezia,* a river which flows through southern Germany. Still another[17] has merely the word *fluvius* with the addition of no name. Although sheer numbers is not a reliable index for the authenticity of the reading *fluvius Sequana* or *fluvius Secana* ("Seine River"), yet this reading is very likely the genuine one, and this is the reading that our printed texts have adopted. Among the manuscripts showing this reading is the Codex Bodleianus 214, which had been in the personal library of Archbishop Robert of Winchelsea (1293-1313), a personage who in all likelihood would have seen that he possessed a carefully copied manuscript. Granted then that *Sequana* is the correct reading, Father Pelster's argument based on the reading *fluvius Renus* would seem to be seriously weakened. Consequently, if this passage has any worth for the controversy and granted that *fluvius Sequana* were words that might have been used appropriately only in Paris, it would seem that *De Spiritualibus Creaturis* originated there, as Father Mandonnet has always sturdily maintained.

But on the other hand M. Grabmann[18] challenged this position on the ground that he had found a manuscript which bore on the margin of *De Spiritualibus Creaturis* the words: *Hic incipiunt questiones fratris Thome d' Aquino disputate in Ytalia.* This he urged in support of the thesis that the series was disputed in Italy. Father Mandonnet,[19] however, in a review of Grabmann's *Indagini e scoperte intorno alla cronologia delle Quaestiones Disputatae,* attacks the assertion on the ground that the last three words of the notation had been written by some other hand than that of the original scribe. In the same review he again cites the passage on the Seine River and inquires with some heat, "Is there a like text that can arise from a disputation held in Italy?"

Still, Father Glorieux[20] very definitely thinks that the evidence of this marginal note plus that of a similar one in another manuscript are to be taken in support of the question's Italian origin. His view is that the work was disputed at Viterbo during the fall of 1262. He upholds his thesis by the following arguments: a) the eleven articles which compose our series correspond to the eleven weeks between the opening of the fall term in September and the time of St. Thomas' departure toward the end of

---

[15] *Op. cit.* p. 232; cf. Birkenmajer, "Kleinere Thomasfragen." *Phil. Jahrb.* XXXIV (1921) pp. 31-49, where this author also inclines to Pelster's view.
[16] Cod. Borghes. 15 (13th or 14th century).
[17] F I 33, cod. 14 of the University of Basle.
[18] *Einführung in die Summa Theologiae des hl. Thomas von Aquin,* p. 23; cf. *Die Werke des hl. Thomas,* pp. 278-279.
[19] *Bulletin Thomiste* I (1924-1926) p. 59.
[20] *Op. cit.,* pp. 5-33.

November, it being the Saint's custom at this time to conduct weekly disputations; b) *De Spiritualibus Creaturis* would seem to be incomplete, something which might be accounted for by the Angelic Doctor's sudden departure for Paris; c) knowing that the Master General of the Dominican order was planning to send him to Paris to do battle with the Averroists, he was working out this particular series of disputations that he might search out data to enable him to take a position on the matter later. Having thus rationalized his stand, Father Glorieux then proceeded to account for the allusion to the Seine in Article X. This he flatly ascribed to a substitution made by the Parisian booksellers out of local pride, since he firmly stated that St. Thomas, because of his sudden departure from Italy, had not time to edit the work at Viterbo and consequently brought it along to Paris, where he edited it and handed it on to the copyists. All of this is logical enough, taking into account as it does known facts of the Saint's life, but the whole chain of reasoning would seem to rest on the acceptance as fact of the authority of three manuscripts.

Besides the highly controversial information that centers around the passage in Article IX, there are three other internal sources that have been employed to shed light on the problem. All are based on quotations from the works of Greek philosophers which were translated into Latin during the adult years of St. Thomas and can thus furnish some indication of the date of composition of *De Spiritualibus Creaturis*. One of these in Article III (Resp.), cites Simplicius' commentary on Aristotle's *Categories*. From the researches of Grabmann[21] we know that this was first made available in Latin through the translation of William of Moerbeke in March 1266. The second (Art. IX, ad 10) quotes from Aristotle's *Politics,* which St. Thomas knew after 1261.[22] The last (Art. X, Resp.) cites Themistius' commentary on Aristotle's *De Anima,* which dates in its Latin version from 1270.[23] This saying, wherein St. Thomas refers to Aristotle according to Themistius as having compared the agent intellect to light, whereas Plato compared it to the sun, is very often used by St. Thomas;[24] although Salman[25] noted the fact and stated that it does not necessarily prove that St. Thomas had already read the commentary. Granted, however, that he had, 1270 would have been the earliest date at which *De Spiritualibus Creaturis* could have been written. However, since this is more or less conjectural, we are thrown back to 1266 as the definite date before which the work could not have been written.

---

[21] *Forschungen über die lateinischen Aristoteles übersetzungen des XIII. Jahrhunderts,* p. 148.
[22] P. Glorieux, *op. cit.,* p. 9.
[23] *Ibid.,* p. 17.
[24] *Summa Theologica* I, q. 89 a. 4; *De Malo* q. 16 a. 12, ad 1; *De Unitate Intellectus* 5, § 120.
[25] *Bulletin Thomiste* (1933) p 1091.

In conclusion, the evidence justifies no more than the following assumptions: that *De Spiritualibus Creaturis* was not written before 1266; that it may have been written in Italy between the years 1266-1268; that it more probably was written in Paris in 1269.

IV. The Value of the *Disputed Questions*

The *Disputed Questions* have long been considered among the important works of St. Thomas. As early as the seventeenth century the Dominican Father Santé Marialès wrote a commentary on them, saying that although he was then eighty years of age and had already spent an entire lifetime in studious pursuits, he had derived more profit from the three or four years of labor on them than he had from what he had accomplished during all the rest of his life.[26] And of recent years Grabmann has considered them "the deepest and most profound work that Thomas has written."[27] Their peculiar value lies in the fact that a given disputed question entered deeply into the discussion of a subject and was not confined to one point of doctrine. In this way a subject could be copiously and profoundly treated. As Dr. Pace[28] has summed up the matter: "This method facilitated analysis and obliged the writer to examine every aspect of the problem. It secured breadth of view and thoroughness of treatment, and was a transparent medium for reason unbiased either by sentiment or verbiage." By reason of their very nature, therefore, they were a sort of work in collaboration with the Angelic Doctor's adversaries, for their objections forced him to solve the difficulties that they brought up against his theories and ideas. This necessity of submitting his thought to severe criticism forced St. Thomas to state his doctrines with the highest precision and coherence. This he might not have achieved had they been the product solely of his own musings.

The topics[29] embraced under the *Disputed Questions* contain a grand total of 510 articles or separate disputations, far more than any other master of the time produced. This was due in no small part to the stormy atmosphere of Paris during the years he spent there. His days as a young professor or master (1256-1259) were days of conflict between the order priests and the seculars over the disposition of the teaching chairs in theology at the University of Paris. This controversy reached its crux when the secular priests withdrew entirely, thus throwing the burden of teaching on the friars. In the face of this difficulty the young master Thomas Aquinas chose to use the disputation at regular and frequent intervals

---

[26] Cited by P. Mandonnet, "Chronologie des Questions Disputées de Saint Thomas d' Aquin." *Revue Thomiste* I (1918) p. 266.
[27] Grabmann, *Die Werke des hl. Thomas*, p. 275.
[28] Pace, E. A., "Thomas Aquinas" in *Library of the World's Best Literature* II, p. 614.
[29] The titles of the separate series are *De Veritate, De Potentia, De Malo, De Unione Verbi Incarnati, De Spiritualibus Creaturis, De Anima, De Virtutibus.*

that he might reach a larger body of listeners. Later in his life when he was recalled from Italy to teach a second time at Paris, he found the city in violent upheaval over the burning questions of Augustinianism and Averroism, and again disputations were held at no long intervals.

But we must not imagine that all the *Disputed Questions* were written in Paris. Some too were held in Italy, for the composition of the whole series extended over the entire teaching career of St. Thomas (1256-1272). In them the materials and doctrines were elaborated which he used more than once later in the composition of the *Summa Theologica.* Because of their regular and successive publication they can furnish the modern scholar with a scale of comparison for the more voluminous works, a scale by means of which we can follow the various phases in the development of the doctrines of St. Thomas.

V. BIBLIOGRAPHY

Birkenmajer, A., "Kleinere Thomasfragen." *Philosophisches Jahrbuch* XXXIV (1921) pp. 31-49.

de Bruyne, Edgar, *S. Thomas d' Aquin.* (Paris, 1928).

Glorieux, P., "Les questions disputées de S. Thomas d' Aquin et leur suite. chronologique." *Recherches de théologie ancienne et médiévale* IV (1932) pp. 5-33.

Grabmann, M., *Forschungen über die Lateinischen Aristoteles-übersetzungen des XIII. Jahrhunderts.* (Münster, 1916).

Grabmann, M., *Thomas Aquinas, His Personality and His Thought,* a translation by Virgil Michel, O.S.B. (New York, 1928).

Grabmann, M., "Beiträge zur Geschichte der Philosophie des Mittelalters." *Baeumker Beiträge* XXII (1930).

Grabmann, M., "Die Werke des hl. Thomas." *Baeumker Beiträge* XXXII (1931).

von Hertling, Georg, "Wo und wann verfasste Thomas von Aquin die Schrift de Spiritualibus Creaturis?" *Historisches Jahrbuch* V (1884) pp. 144-145.

Hourcade, René, "Des écrits authentiques de Saint Thomas d' Aquin." *Bulletin de littérature ecclésiastique* (1912) pp. 175-180.

Mandonnet, P., "Chronologie des Questions disputées de Saint Thomas d' Aquin." *Revue Thomiste* I (1918) pp. 266-287.

Mandonnet, P., "Chronologie sommaire de la vie et des écrits de S. Thomas." *Revue des sciences philosophiques et théologiques* IX (1920) pp. 148 ff.

Mandonnet, P., A review of M. Grabmann's *Indagini e scoperte intorno alla cronologia delle Quaestiones Disputatae e Quodlibeta di S. Tommaso. Bulletin Thomiste* I (1924-1926) pp. 58-61.

Mandonnet, P., *Quaestiones Disputatae,* Introduction, vol. I, pp. 1-24, (Paris, 1925).

Pelster, F., "Der Katalog des Bartholomaeus von Capua und die Echtheitsfragen bei den Schriften des hl. Thomas." *Zeitschrift für katolische Theologie* XLI (1917) pp. 820-832.

Pelster, F., "Zur Datierung des Qu. dis. De Spiritualibus Creaturis." *Gregorianum* VI (1925) pp. 231-247.

Sertillanges, A., *S. Thomas d' Aquin.* (Paris, 1925).

Synave, P., *Bulletin Thomiste* I (1924-1926) pp. 1-21.

Synave, P., "Le Probléme chronologique des Questions Disputées de S. Thomas d' Aquin." *Revue Thomiste* XXXI (1926) pp. 154-159.

On Spiritual Creatures

THE TOPIC TO BE INVESTIGATED IS
CONCERNING SPIRITUAL CREATURES

[handwritten: What's a "spiritual substance"? angel? man?]

ARTICLE I

AND the first question is: Whether a spiritual substance is composed of matter and form.[1]

And it would seem that it is. *1* For Boethius says in his book *De Trinitate* [II, *Patrologia Latina* LXIV, 1250 D] : A simple form cannot be a subject. But a created spiritual substance is a subject of knowledge and of power and of grace; therefore, it is not a simple form. But neither is it simple matter, for in that case it would exist in potency only, and would have no activity. Therefore it is composed of matter and form.

2 Furthermore, any created form is limited and finite. But form is limited through matter. Therefore, any created form is a form in matter. Therefore no created substance is a form without matter.

3 Furthermore, the principle of changeability is matter; hence, according to the Philosopher [*Metaphysica* II, 2, 994b 26], "it is necessary that matter be conceived[2] in a thing that is moved." But a created spiritual substance is changeable; for only God is by nature unchangeable. Therefore a created spiritual substance has matter.

4 Furthermore, Augustine says in XII *Confessiones* [17, 25] that God made matter common to things visible and things invisible. Now the things invisible are spiritual substances. Therefore a spiritual substance has matter.

5 Furthermore, the Philosopher says in VIII *Metaphysica* [6, 1045a 36] that if any substance is without matter, it is at once both being

---

[1] Cf. *De Ente et Essentia* 5; *In I Sent.* d. 8, q. 5, a. 2 (on the soul); *In II Sent.** d. 3, q. 1, a. 1 (on the angels); d. 17, q. 1, a. 2 (on the soul): *In Boethium De Trinitate* 5, a. 4, ad 4; *In Boeth. De Hebdomadibus* lec. 2; *Summa Contra Gentiles* II, cap. 50, 51; *De Potentia* VI, 6, ad 4; *Quodl.* IX, a. 6 (on the angels); *Summa Theologica* I, q. 50, a. 2 (on the angels); q. 75, a. 5 (on the soul); *Q. De Anima** 6; *De Subst. Separatis* 5-8; *Quodl.* III, a. 20 (on the soul); *De Sp. Cr.* art. 9, ad 9. (Passages marked with an asterisk should be read before the others).

Avicebron, *Fons vitae,* tr. 4, and elsewhere *passim;* Philippus Cancellarius, q. i. *De An.;* Guilelmus Alvernus, *De Universo* II, 2, c. 7 et sqq.; *De An.* III, 1; Joannes de Rupella *De An.* I, c. 13; Alexander Halensis, *Summa* II, 1, p. 398; S. Bonaventura, II *Sent.,* d. 3, p. 89; Albertus M., II *Sent.,* d. 3, vol. 27, p. 66; *Summa Theol.* II, tr. 1, q. 3, vol. 32, pp. 33, 38; *Summa Philosophiae,* tr. 10, cc. 6, 7; Roger Bacon, *Communia Natur.* IV, 3, c. 4 pp. 291-294.

On the history of the problem, cf. E. Kleineidam, *Das Problem der hylomorphen Zusammensetzung der geistigen Substanzen im* 13 *Jahrh. behandelt bis zu Th. von Aquin,* Liebenthal, 1930; O. Lottin, "La compos. hylemorphique des substances spirituelles." *Revue Néo-Scolastique,* XXXIV (1932), pp. 21-44. Both writers give texts previously published.

[2] St. Thomas usually quotes the Arabic version of this statement, in which "ut imaginetur" is given for νοεῖν; cf. *In I Sent.* I, d. 17, q. 1, a. 2.

[15]

and one *(ens et unum)*, and there is no other cause for it to be both being and one. But everything that has been created has a cause of its being and of its unity. Therefore no created thing is substance without matter. Therefore, every created spiritual substance is composed of matter and form.

6   Furthermore, Augustine[3] says in his book *De Quaestionibus Veteris et Novi Testamenti* [q. 23, *PL* XXXV, 2229] that Adam's body was formed before the soul was infused into it, because a dwelling must be made before a dweller is introduced. Now the soul is related to the body as a dweller to a dwelling; but a dweller has a subsistence of its own: the soul accordingly has a subsistence of its own, and, for all the greater reason, an angel. But a substance with a subsistence of its own does not seem to be merely a form. Therefore a created spiritual substance is not merely a form; it is, therefore, composed of matter and form.

7   Furthermore, it is manifest that the soul is able to take on contraries. Now this would seem to be a property of a composite substance. Therefore the soul is a composite substance, and by the same reasoning so is an angel.

8   Furthermore, form is that whereby a thing is *(quo aliquid est)*. Whatever, therefore, is composed of that whereby it is and of that which it is *(quo et quod est)* is composed of matter and form. Now every created spiritual substance is composed of that whereby it is and of that which it is, as Boethius[4] makes clear in his book *De Hebdomadibus* [*PL* LXIV, 1311]. Therefore, every created spiritual substance is composed of matter and form.

9   Furthermore, there are two kinds of "commonness" *(duplex communitas)* : one, in the divine order, whereby the essence is "common" to the three persons; another, in the created order, whereby the universal is "common" to the things that come under it *(suis inferioribus)*. Now it would seem to be a peculiarity of the first sort of "commonness" that the feature which makes a difference between those beings which share the common element is not really anything else than the common element itself. For the paternity by which the Father is different from the Son is itself the essence which is common to the Father and to the Son. Now in the "commonness" of the universal the feature that makes a difference between the things which are included under the common element must

---

[3] On this apocryphal work, see *Dictionnaire de théologie catholique,* Art. "S. Augustin," 2308.
[4] Boethius makes a distinction between "that which is" *(quod est)* and "being" *(esse);* but Gilbert de la Porrée in his commentary introduced the distinction between "that which is" and "that whereby something is" *(quo est),* which the mediaeval philosophers used to attribute to Boethius himself. Compare the cautious wording in *Sum. Theol.* I, q. 75, a. 5, ad 4: "And hence (a spirit) is said by some men to be composed of that whereby a thing is and of that which is; for being *(esse)* itself is that whereby a thing is."

be something else than the common element itself. In every created thing, therefore, which is included in a common genus there necessarily is a composition of the common element and of that whereby the common element itself is restricted. Now a created spiritual substance is in a given genus. Therefore in a created spiritual substance there must be composition of the common nature and of that whereby the common nature is confined. Now this seems to be a composition of form and of matter. Therefore in a created spiritual substance there is composition of form and of matter.

10 Furthermore, the form of a genus cannot exist save in the intellect or in matter. But a created spiritual substance, such as an angel, is in a given genus. Accordingly, the form of that genus exists either in the intellect only, or in matter. But if an angel did not possess matter, it would not exist in matter. Therefore it would exist in the intellect only, and so, supposing that nobody had intellectual knowledge of an angel, it would follow that the angel did not exist. This is an incongruity *(inconveniens)*. Accordingly, it is necessary to say (as it seems) that created spiritual substance is composed of matter and form.

11 Furthermore, if a created spiritual substance were merely form, it would follow that one spiritual substance would be present to another. For if one angel has intellectual knowledge of another, either this happens through the essence of the understood angel, and in this case it will be necessary for the substance of the understood angel to be present in the intellect of the angel understanding it; or else it happens through a species, and in that case the same conclusion follows, if the species through which the angel is understood by the other angel does not differ from the very substance of the understood angel. Nor does it seem possible to indicate anything wherein it does differ, if the substance of the angel is without matter, as is its intelligible species also. Now this latter is an incongruity, that one angel should be present in another by its own substance, because it is only the Trinity that enters into the rational mind *(menti rationali illabitur)*. Therefore the first point too, from which this follows, is incongruous; namely, that a created spiritual substance is immaterial.

12 Furthermore, the Commentator says in XI *Metaphysica* [XII, comm. 36] that if there were a box[5] without matter, it would be the same as the box which exists in the intellect. Consequently the conclusion seems the same as before.

13 Augustine says in VII *Super Genesi ad Litteram* [6, 9] that, just as the flesh had matter (that is, earth) from which it was made, so perhaps it might have been the case that, even before that very nature

---

[5] In the passage cited the Commentator speaks of "a bath" in nature and in the intellect; and he does not bring in the example of the box in that book.

[17]

which is called the soul was made, it had as its own genus a kind of spiritual matter, which was not yet a soul. Therefore the soul seems to be composed of matter and form, and by the same reasoning an angel also.

14 Furthermore, Damascene says [De Fide Orthodoxa II, 3 & 12, Patrologia Graeca XCIV, 867 and 919] that "God alone is essentially immaterial and incorporeal." Therefore a created spiritual substance is not immaterial and incorporeal.

15 Furthermore, every substance circumscribed by the limits of its own nature has a limited and confined existence. But every created substance is circumscribed by the limits of its own nature. Therefore every created substance has a limited and confined existence. But every thing which is confined is confined by something. Therefore in any and every created substance there is a confining element and a confined element; and these seem to be matter and form. Therefore every spiritual substance is composed of matter and form.

16 Furthermore, nothing is active and passive on the same basis, but each thing is active through its form, whereas it is passive through its matter.[6] But a created spiritual substance, such as an angel, is active while it is enlightening a lower angel and is passive while it is being enlightened by a higher angel. Similarly, there is in the soul the agent intellect (intellectus agens) and the possible intellect (intellectus possibilis). Therefore an angel as well as the soul is composed of matter and form.

17 Furthermore, every thing that is either is a pure act or a pure potency, or is something composed of act and potency. But a spiritual substance is not a pure act (for this is characteristic of God alone), nor is it a pure potency either. Therefore it is something composed of potency and act, which seems the same as something composed of matter and form.

18 Furthermore, Plato in the Timaeus [13, 41 AB] introduces the highest god as saying, when speaking to the created gods: "My will is greater than your bond." Augustine quotes these words in his book De Civitate Dei [XIII, 16, 1]. Now the created gods seem to be angels. Therefore in angels there is a bond or composition.

19 Furthermore, in those things which are counted, and are different in essence, there is matter; because matter is the principle of numerical distinction. But spiritual substances are counted, and are different in essence. Therefore they have matter.

20 Furthermore, nothing is acted on by a body except a thing that has matter. But created spiritual substances are acted on by bodily fire, as

---

[6] Cf. Q. De An. 6, resp., where the main argument of the adversaries is expressed as follows: "that in whatever thing the properties of matter are found, matter must be found. And hence, since the properties of matter are found in the soul, which are receiving, being a subject, being in potency, and others of the sort, he thinks it necessary for matter to be in the soul."

[18]

angels have substance - what?

Augustine makes clear in *De Civitate Dei* [XXI, 10]. Therefore created spiritual substances have matter.

21   Furthermore, Boethius in his book *De Unitate et Uno* [*PL* LXIII, 1076-77] expressly says that an angel is composed of matter and form.

22   Furthermore, Boethius says in his book *De Hebdomadibus* [*PL* LXIII, 1311] that that which is can have something else mixed with it. But existence itself has absolutely nothing else mixed with it; and we can say the same about all abstract and concrete things. For in man there can be something other than "humanity", such as "whiteness" or something of that sort; but in "humanity" itself there can be nothing other than what pertains to the character of "humanity". If, therefore, spiritual substances are abstract forms, there will not possibly be in them anything that does not pertain to their species. But if something that pertains to the species of a thing be taken away, the thing is corrupted. Since, therefore, every spiritual substance is incorruptible, nothing that is in a created spiritual substance will possibly be lost; and so it will be utterly immobile, which is incongruous.

vs. Platonic forms?

23   Furthermore, every thing which is in a genus participates in the principles of the genus. Now a created spiritual substance is in the category of substance. Now the principles of this category are matter and form, as Boethius makes clear in his *Commentum Praedicamentorum* [*PL* LXIV, 184], where he says that Aristotle, leaving out of consideration the extremes, namely, matter and form, discusses the mean, namely, the composite; and gives us to understand that the substance, which is the category about which he is speaking in that passage, is composed of matter and form. Therefore a created spiritual substance is composed of of matter and form.

24   Furthermore, every thing which is in a genus is composed of genus and difference. Now the difference is obtained from the form, whereas the genus is obtained from the matter, as he makes clear in VIII *Metaphysica* [2, 1043a 19; 3, 1043b 30]. Since, then, a spiritual substance is in a genus, it seems that it is composed of matter and form.

25   Furthermore, that which is first in any genus whatever is the cause of the things which are subsequent;[7] as for instance, the first act is the cause of every being that is in act. Therefore by the same reasoning every thing that is in potency in any way whatever has this character from the first potency which is pure potency, namely, from prime matter. But there is some potency in created spiritual substances, because God alone is pure act. Therefore a created spiritual substance has this character from matter; which could not be so unless matter were a part of it. Therefore it is composed of matter and form.

---

[7] The Scholastics frequently quote this statement as though it were Aristotle's; cf. *Met.* II, 1, 993b 24; *Met.* X, 2, 1053b.

[19]

But on the other hand *i* there is what Dionysius says in chapter IV of *De Divinis Nominibus* [lec. 1] about the angels, that they are "incorporeal and immaterial."

But you will say that *ii* they are called "immaterial" because they do not have matter that is subject to quantity and to change. But this is at variance with what he himself says above, that "they are free from all matter."

iii Furthermore, according to the Philosopher in IV *Physica* [4, 211a 12], the question of place would not arise were it not for movement; and similarly neither would the question of matter arise were it not for movement. Therefore, according as given things have movement, on this ground matter must be looked for in them; hence those things which are subject to generation and corruption have matter with respect to their being; while those which are changeable according to place have matter with respect to their place. But spiritual substances are not changeable on the basis of their being. Therefore matter for being is not in them, and so they are not composed of matter and form.

iv Furthermore, Hugh of St. Victor says on Dionysius' *De Caelesti Hierarchia* [V, PL CLXXV, 1010B], that in spiritual substances that which vivifies and that which is vivified is the same. But that which vivifies is form, whereas that which is vivified is matter; for form gives being to matter, and in the case of living things "to live" is "to be". Therefore in angels there is no distinction of matter and form.

v Furthermore, Avicenna [*Met.* IX, 4] and Algazel [I, tr. IV, 3] say that the separated substances, which are called spiritual substances, are entirely devoid of matter.

vi Furthermore, the Philosopher says in III *De Anima* [8, 431b 29] that "the stone does not exist in the soul, but the species" of stone does. This seems to be due to the soul's simplicity, namely, the fact that material things cannot exist in it. Therefore the soul is not composed of matter and form.

vii Furthermore, in the *Liber de Causis* [§6] it is said that an intelligence is a substance which is not divided. But every thing which is composite is divided. Therefore an intelligence is not composite substance.

viii Furthermore, "in those things which are without matter, the understanding being and the understood being are the same" [III *De An.*, 4, 430a 3]. But that which is understood is an entirely immaterial intelligible form. Therefore the understanding substance also is without matter.

ix Furthermore, Augustine says in his book *De Trinitate* [IX, 4], that the whole soul understands itself. Now it does not understand through matter: therefore matter is not a part of it *(aliquid eius)*.

[20]

x Furthermore, Damascene says [*De Fide Orth*. II, 12] that the soul is simple. Therefore it is not composed of matter and form.

xi Furthermore, a rational soul more closely approaches the absolutely simple First Being (namely, God) than the animal soul *(spiritus brutalis)* does. But the animal soul is not composed of matter and form. Therefore much less is the rational soul.

xii Furthermore, the angelic substance more closely approaches the simple First Being than a material form does.[8] But a material form is not composed of matter and form. Therefore, neither is the angelic substance.

xiii Furthermore, accidental form is below substance in the order of importance. But God makes a given accidental form subsist without matter, as is evident in the Sacrament of the Altar. Therefore, so much the more does He make a given form in the genus of substance subsist without matter; and this especially seems to be spiritual substance.

xiv Furthermore, Augustine says in XII *Confessiones* [7]: You have made two things, O Lord, "one next to Yourself", that is, angelic substance, "another next to nothing", namely, matter. So, therefore, there is no matter in an angel, since "matter" is distinguished from "angel" as its contrary.

ANSWER. There are a variety of conflicting opinions concerning this question. For some assert that a created spiritual substance is a composite of matter and form; but some deny this. And hence, in order not to proceed to the investigation of this truth in an ambiguous fashion, we must consider what is meant by the term "matter." For it is obvious that since potency and act are divisions of being *(ens)*, and since any genus whatever is divided into potency and act, the term "prime matter" is generally used to mean something which is in the genus of substance as a kind of potency, which is understood as excluding every species and form, and even as excluding privation, and yet is a potency capable of receiving both forms and privations; as Augustine makes clear in XII *Confessiones* [vii, viii, xv] and in I *Super Genesi ad Litteram* [xiv, xv], and the Philosopher in VII *Metaphysica* [3, 1029a 20].

Now if matter be taken in this sense, which is its proper and generally accepted meaning, it is impossible for matter to be in spiritual substances.

---

[8] These are the arguments which St. Thomas everywhere emphasizes. In *In II Sent.*, d. 17, the *responsio* begins as follows: "It must be said that matter does not seem to me to be in the soul or in any spiritual substance in any way . . . although some say otherwise"; in *De Pot*. VI, 6, ad 4: "Yet I believe rather that the angels are not composed of matter and form." But in the later works he attacks his adversaries more sharply, perhaps because he is more strongly of the opinion that their doctrine takes its origin from Avicebron; cf. the unusual vehemence of *Q. De. An*. 6: "But this reasoning is frivolous and the position impossible;" "It is obvious that the reasoning mentioned above is frivolous"; "and this is utterly absurd", etc.

For although in one and the same given thing which is sometimes in act and sometimes in potency, potency is prior to act in the order of time, yet in the order of nature act is prior to potency.[9] Now that which is prior does not depend on that which is subsequent, but vice versa. And consequently one comes upon a first act in isolation from all potency; yet one never finds in nature a potency which is not perfected by some act, and on this account there is always some form in prime matter. Now the first absolutely perfect act, which has in itself all the fullness of perfection, causes actual existence in all things; but yet according to a certain order. For no caused act has all the fullness of perfection, but in comparison with the first act every caused act is imperfect. Still, the more perfect an act is, the nearer it is to God. Now of all creatures, the spiritual substances are nearest to God, as Dionysius makes clear in chapter 4 of *De Caelesti Hierarchia* [§1]. And hence they most nearly approach the perfection of the first act, since they are related to lower creatures as the perfect is to the imperfect and as act is to potency. Therefore the ordered scheme of things does not in any sense imply that spiritual substances, for their own actual being, need prime matter, which is the most incomplete of all beings; but they are on a level that is far above all matter and all material things.

This fact also becomes evident if one takes into consideration the activity that is proper to spiritual substances. For all spiritual substances are intellectual. Now the potency of each individual thing is such as its perfection is found to be; for a proper act requires its own proper potency. Now the perfection of any intellectual substance, insofar as it is intellectual, is intelligible because it is in the intellect. The sort of potency then that we must seek in spiritual substances is one that is proportionate to the reception of an intelligible form. Now the potency of prime matter is not of this sort, for prime matter receives form by contracting it to the individual being. But an intelligible form is in the intellect without any such contraction; for thus the intellect understands each intelligible as its form is in it. Now the intellect understands the intelligible chiefly according to a common and universal nature, and so the intelligible form is in the intellect according to its universality *(secundum rationem suae communitatis)*. Therefore, an intellectual substance is not made receptive of form by reason of prime matter, but rather through a character which is, in a way, the opposite. Hence it becomes obvious that in the case of spiritual substances the kind of prime matter which of itself is void of all species cannot be part of that substance.

Yet on the other hand if we use the terms "matter" and "form" to mean any two things which are related to each other as potency and act,

---

[9] Cf. Aristotle, IX *Met.,* 8, 1049b, with St. Thomas' commentary, lec. 7.

there is no difficulty in saying (so as to avoid a mere dispute about words) that matter and form exist in spiritual substances. For in a created spiritual substance there must be two elements, one of which is related to the other as potency is to act. This is clear from the following. For it is obvious that the first being, which is God, is infinite act, as having in itself the entire fullness of being, not contracted to any generic or specific nature. Hence its very existence must not be an existence that is, as it were, put into some nature which is not its own existence, because thus it would be limited to that nature. Hence we say that God is His own existence. Now this cannot be said of any other being. For, just as it is impossible to understand that there are many separate whitenesses, but if there were "whiteness" apart from every subject and recipient, there would be but one whiteness, so it is impossible to have a self-subsisting existence unless there is but one. Accordingly, every thing which exists after the first being, because it is not its own existence, has an existence that is received in something, through which the existence is itself contracted; and thus in any created object the nature of the thing which participates in existence is one thing, and the participated existence itself is another. And because any thing participates in the first act through similitude insofar as it has existence, the participated existence must in each case be related to the nature participating in it, as act is related to potency. Accordingly, in the world of physical objects, matter does not of itself participate in actual existence, but it does participate therein through form; for the form coming upon the matter makes the matter itself actually exist, as the soul does to the body.

Hence in composite objects there are two kinds of act and two kinds of potency to consider. For first of all, matter is as potency with reference to form, and the form is its act. And secondly, if the nature is constituted of matter and form, the matter is as potency with reference to existence itself, insofar as it is able to receive this. Accordingly, when the foundation of matter is removed, if any form of a determinate nature remains which subsists of itself but not in matter, it will still be related to its own existence as potency is to act. But I do not say, as that potency which is separable from its act, but as a potency which is always accompanied by its act. And in this way the nature of a spiritual substance, which is not composed of matter and form, is a potency with reference to its own existence; and thus there is in a spiritual substance a composition of potency and act, and, consequently, of form and matter, provided only that every potency be called matter, and every act be called form; but yet this is not properly said according to the common use of the terms.[10]

---

[10] St. Thomas is less tolerant with such an improper mode of expression in Q. De An. 6, resp.: "And hence matter is not found except in corporeal things in the sense in which philosophers have spoken of matter, unless one wishes to take

[23]

As to the first argument, therefore, it must be said that the character of a form is in sharp contrast to the character of a subject: for every form, as such, is an act, whereas every subject is related to that of which it is the subject, as a potency is related to an act. If therefore, there is any form which is exclusively an act, such as the divine essence, it cannot in any sense be a subject; and it is of this form that Boethius is speaking. Now if there happens to be a form, which is in act in one respect and is in potency in another, it will be a subject only in that precise respect in which it is in potency. Now spiritual substances, although they are subsistent forms, are nevertheless in potency inasmuch as they possess a finite and limited existence. And because the intellect, as a consequence of its character, has a capacity for knowing all things, and the will has a capacity for loving all good, there always remains within the intellect and the will of a created substance a potency toward something which is outside of itself. Hence, if one views the matter rightly, spiritual substances are not found to be subjects, except of accidents which pertain to the intellect and to the will.

As to the second, it must be said that there are two kinds of limitation of form. There is one in consequence of which the form of the species is limited to the individual, and this kind of limitation of form comes about through matter. There is a second, however, in consequence of which the form of the genus is limited to the nature of the species; and this kind of limitation of form does not come about through matter, but rather through a more determinate form, from which the difference is derived; for the difference when added to a genus narrows down this latter to the species. And this kind of limitation is the one that is in spiritual substances, in view of the fact that they are forms of determinate species.

As to the third, it must be said that changeability is not to be found in spiritual substances as a consequence of their being, but as a consequence of their intellect and their will. But this kind of changeability is not the result of matter, but of the potentiality of the intellect and the will.

As to the fourth, it must be said that Augustine's meaning is not that the matter of things visible and things invisible is the same numerically; since he himself says that two kinds of formlessness are meant by "heaven" and "earth," which are said to have been created first, so that by "heaven" is meant the spiritual substance that is still formless, whereas by "earth" is meant the matter of corporeal objects, which considered in itself is formless, since it is without any species; hence it is also said to

---

matter equivocally", but if one does, "he is obviously deceived in consequence of the equivocation". Cf. below, Art. 9, ad 9: "nothing prevents someone else from calling matter what we call act; just as, for instance, what we call stone someone else can call ass."

be "void and empty", or "invisible and non-composite" according to another reading, whereas heaven is not described as "void and empty." From this it is plainly manifest that matter, which is without any species, is not a part of the angelic substance. But the formlessness of spiritual substance is a consequence of the fact that the substance has not yet been turned toward the Word whereby it is enlightened, and this is something that pertains to its power of understanding.[11] In this sense, therefore, he calls them both "common matter of things visible and things invisible," according as each is formless in its own way.

As to the fifth, it must be said that the Philosopher is speaking in that passage not of the agent cause but of the formal cause. For those things which are composed of matter and form are not immediately both being and one, but matter is being in potency and becomes actual being through the coming of the form, which serves as the cause of existence in its regard. But a form does not have being through another form. And hence, if there be a subsisting form, it is immediately both being and one, nor does it have a formal cause of its own existence; it does nevertheless have a cause that pours existence into it, but not a moving cause such as would bring it into act out of previously existent potency.

As to the sixth, it must be said that, although the soul has a subsistence of its own, nevertheless it does not follow that it is composed of matter and form, because to have a subsistence of its own can also be an attribute of a form apart from matter. For since matter has existence through form, and not conversely, there is nothing to prevent a given form from subsisting without matter, although matter cannot exist without form.

As to the seventh, it must be said that the capacity of receiving contrary attributes is characteristic of a substance that exists in potency in some way or other, whether it be composed of matter and form or whether it be simple substance. Now the substance of spiritual things is not the subject of contrary attributes, save of those pertaining to the will and to the intellect, since it is in consequence of these that it is in potency, as is clear from what has been said.

As to the eighth, it must be said that to be composed of "that which is" *(quod est)* and of "that whereby something is" *(quo est)* is not the same as to be composed of matter and form.[12] For although form can be called "that whereby something is," nevertheless matter cannot properly be called "that which is," since it is not, save in potency. But "that which is" is that which subsists in existence and this, in the case of corporeal substances, is the thing itself that is composed of matter and

---

[11] Cf. Augustine, *De Genesi ad Litteram* I, 1, 2-3.

[12] *In I Sent.* d. 8, q. 5, a. 2, resp., there is the explanation of how "in compounds of matter and form that whereby something is can be said in three senses"; and in *Contra Gentiles* II, cap. 52-54, the question of "that which is" and "that whereby something is" is discussed at length.

[25]

form, whereas in the case of incorporeal substances it is the simple form itself. Now "that whereby something is" is participated existence itself, because each individual is, insofar as it participates in existence itself. And hence Boethius also uses these words in this sense in the book *De Hebdomadibus,* saying that in the case of beings other than the First "that which is" and "existence" *(esse)* are not the same.

As to the ninth, it must be said that a thing is "under" something common in two senses: in one, as an individual is "under" a species; in another, as a species is "under" a genus. Whenever then many individuals are under one common species, the distinction between many individuals is effected through individual matter, which has nothing to do with their specific nature. This is true in the case of created things. But when there are many species under one genus the forms whereby the species are distinguished from one another should in reality be something other than the common form of the genus. For through one and the same form this particular individual is put in the genus "substance", in the genus "body", and so on down to the most specific species.[13] For if this particular individual were to possess its substantiality in consequence of some form, then necessarily it would have to be the case that the other additional forms in consequence of which it is placed in lower genera and species would be accidental forms.

This is clear from the following. For an accidental form differs from a substantial form because a substantial form makes this given thing to be something, whereas an accidental form is added to a thing which already exists as "this something." If then the first form by which the individual is placed in a genus will make the individual to be "this something," all the other forms will be added to an individual that subsists in actuality, and consequently they will be accidental forms. It will also follow that through the addition of the later forms whereby something is given its place in the most specific species or in some subordinate species, generation does not occur, and by the taking away of these forms there is no corruption in an absolute sense but in a qualified sense *(secundum aliquid).* For since generation is a change oriented to the existence of a thing, something is said to be generated, absolutely speaking, if it absolutely becomes a being *(ens)* out of that which is non-being in act but being in potency only. If, then, something comes into being out of something that is previously existing in act, what will be generated is not a being in an absolute sense, but "this particular being." Concerning corruption the same reasoning holds good. It must, therefore, be said that the

---

[13] Cf. G. Théry, "L'augustinisme mediéval et le probl. de l'unité de la forme substantielle," *Acta hebdom. Augus. -thom.* (Rome, 1931) pp. 140-200; yet in this article the well-known author unduly restricts the problem to the question of the vegetative, the sentient, and the intellectual soul in man.

forms of things are ranged in order, and that one form exceeds another *hierarchy number* in perfection. This is clear both from what the Philosopher says in VIII *Metaphysica* [3, 1043b 33], namely, that the definitions and species of things are like numbers, in the case of which the species are multiplied by adding one; and also from the fact that through induction the species of things appear to be multiplied hierarchically according to the perfect and the imperfect.

Thus, then, by this line of argument Avicebron's[14] position in the book *Fons Vitae* is ruled out, to the effect that prime matter, something that is regarded as entirely without form, first receives the form of substance; and once this form is supposed in any part of itself it receives, in addition to the form "substance", another form through which it becomes a body; and so on in succession down to its ultimate species. And in that part in which it does not receive a corporeal form it is incorporeal substance, the matter of which, not being subject to quantity, some call "spiritual matter". Moreover, the matter itself, already perfected through the form of substance which is the subject of quantity and of the other accidents, is "the key", he says, to the understanding of incorporeal substances [II, 6, p. 35]. For the reason why some individual thing happens to be a non-living body and another happens to be a living body is not the fact that a living individual has some form of which the substantial form of a body is a substratum; but the reason is that this particular living individual has a more perfect form, through which it has not only subsistence and bodily existence, but also life; whereas the other has a more imperfect form, through which it does not attain to life, but only to bodily existence.

As to the tenth, it must be said that the form of a genus whereof matter is an essential part cannot exist outside the intellect except in matter, like the form "plant", for instance, or the form "metal". But this genus of substance is not the sort of thing whereof matter is an essential part. Otherwise it would not be a metaphysical genus but a natural one. Hence the form of this genus does not depend on matter as regards its own existence, but can be also found outside matter.

As to the eleventh, it must be said that the intelligible species which is in the intellect of the understanding angel is different from the understood angel, not in the way of "something abstracted from the matter" and "something concreted of matter", but as an intentional being differs from a being which has an established existence in nature, as the species of color in the eye differs from the color which is in a wall.

---

[14] Cf. below, Art. 3, resp. In *De Ente et Essen.* 5 and *In II Sent.*, d. 3 St. Thomas says hesitantly: "The author of this position seems to have been Avicebron;" this doubt later disappears. He often states and refutes the doctrine of that Hebrew philosopher (Salomon ben Gebirol, fl. 1050, whom the mediaeval philosophers believed to be an Arab), especially in *De Subst. Separatis*, cc. 5-8 and 10.

As to the twelfth, it must be said that if the box were self-subsistent apart from matter, it would be something that understands its own self, because immunity from matter is the essential character of intellectuality. And in view of this, the box apart from matter would not be different from an intelligible box.

As to the thirteenth, it must be said that Augustine brings in that point as a matter to be investigated. This is clear from the fact that he rejects the assertion in question.

As to the fourteenth, it must be said that God alone is said to be immaterial and incorporeal, because all things, when compared to His simplicity, can be reckoned as material bodies, although in themselves they are incorporeal and immaterial.

As to the fifteenth, it must be said that the existence of a spiritual creature's substance is confined and limited, not by matter, but by the fact that it is something that has been received and participated in a nature of a determinate species, as has been said.

As to the sixteenth, it must be said that a created spiritual substance is active and passive, not in consequence of form or matter, but according as it is in act or in potency.

As to the seventeenth, it must be said that a spiritual substance is neither a pure act nor a pure potency, but is something that has potency along with act; yet it is not composed of matter and form, as is clear from what has been said.

As to the eighteenth, it must be said that Plato gives the name of "second gods" not to the angels, but to the heavenly bodies.

As to the nineteenth, it must be said that matter is the principle of numerical distinction within the same species, but not of the distinction between species. Now the angels are not numerically many within the same species, but their manyness *(multitudo)* is that of many self-subsistent specific natures.

As to the twentieth, it must be said that spiritual substances are not acted on by bodily fire by way of a material alteration but by way of a confinement *(alligationis)*, as Augustine says [*De Civitate Dei* XXI, 10, 1]. And hence it is not necessary for them to have matter.

As to the twenty-first, it must be said that the book *De Unitate et Uno* is not a book of Boethius,[15] as its very style indicates.

As to the twenty-second, it must be said that a separated form, inasmuch as it is an act, cannot have anything extraneous mixed with it, but only inasmuch as it is in potency. And in this way the spiritual substances, inasmuch as they are in potency as regards the intellect and the will, receive some accidents.

---

[15] Its real author was Dominic Gundisalvus Segoviensis (ca. 1150) ; see P. Correns, *Baeumker Beiträge* I, 1, (1891).

[28]

As to the twenty-third, it must be said that Boethius does not mean to say that it is essential to substance, which is a genus, to be composed of matter and form, since substance comes within the purview of the metaphysician, not of the natural philosopher. But he does mean to say that, since form and matter do not pertain to the genus of substance as a species thereof, only that substance which is something composite is placed within the genus of substance as a species.

As to the twenty-fourth, it must be said that in the case of objects composed of matter and form, the genus is obtained from the matter and the difference from the form: yet in such a way that by "matter" is not understood prime matter, but matter according as it receives through the form a certain being *(esse)*, imperfect and material in comparison with specific being *(esse)*; thus, for instance, the being *(esse)* of "animal" is imperfect and material in comparison with "man." Still that two-fold being *(esse)* is not the consequence of two different forms, but of one form, which confers on man not only "animal being" *(esse)* but "human being" *(esse)*. Now the soul of another animal confers on it only "animal being" *(esse)*. Hence the common element "animal" is not one numerically, but mentally only, because it is not from one and the same form that a man and an ass are "animal". Once matter is taken away, therefore, from spiritual substances, the genus and the difference will remain in them, not in consequence of matter and form, but in consequence of considering in a spiritual substance both that element which is common to itself and to less perfect substances, and also that element which is proper to itself.

As to the twenty-fifth, it must be said that the more a thing is in act, the more perfect it is; whereas the more a thing is in potency, the less perfect it is. Now, imperfect beings derive their origin from perfect beings, and not conversely. And hence it does not have to be the case that every thing which is in potency in any way whatever must get its potentiality from the pure potency which is matter. And on this point Avicebron seems to have been deceived, in his book *Fons Vitae*, since he believed that every thing which is in potency, or is a subject, has this character somehow from prime matter.

Spiritual substances are not composed of matter + form

[29]

THE second question is: Can a spiritual substance be united to a body?[1] if so, how? as a form? as intellect?

And it would seem that it cannot. *1* For Dionysius says in the first chapter of *De Divinis Nominibus* [lec. 1] that incorporeal things cannot be completely grasped by corporeal things. But every form is completely grasped by matter, since it is its act. Therefore, an incorporeal spiritual substance cannot be the form of the body.

2 Furthermore, according to the Philosopher in his book *De Somno et Vigilia* [I, 454a 8], "The thing to which an action belongs is the thing to which the corresponding power belongs." But understanding is the proper activity of a spiritual substance and cannot belong to the body, because understanding does not take place through a corporeal organ, as is proved in III *De Anima* [4, 429a 25]. Therefore, an intellectual power cannot be the form of the body; therefore neither can a spiritual substance, wherein this sort of power has its basis, be the form of the body.

3 Furthermore, what accrues to a thing after its completed being *(esse)* accrues to it accidentally. But a spiritual substance has within itself subsistent being *(esse)*. If, then, a body accrues to it, it will accrue to it accidentally. Therefore, it cannot be united to it as a substantial form.

But it was objected[2] that the soul, insofar as it is "spirit", is self-subsistent, whereas insofar as it is "soul", it is united as a form. But on the contrary, *4* the soul is "spirit" by its very essence: accordingly, it is the form of the body either by its very essence or else in consequence of something added to its essence. Now if the soul is the form of the body in consequence of something added to its essence, since all that accrues to a thing over and above its own essence is accidental, it follows that the soul is united to the body by means of some accident; and thus man is a being *per accidens,* which is incongruous. Therefore, the soul is united to the body through its essence, insofar as it is "spirit".

---

[1] *In II Sent.,* d. 1, q. 2, a. 4; d. 17, q. 2, a. 1; *Contra Gentiles* II,* cap. 56, 57, 68, 69, 70; *Sum. Theol.** I, q. 76, a. 1; *Q. De An.,* 1-2; *In II De An.,* lec. 4 (271-277); *In III De An.,* lec. 7 (689-699); *De Unitate Intellectus,* c. 3; *Compendium Theologiae* 80; 87.
　　Aristotle, *De An.* II, cc. 2-3; III, c. 4. Avicenna *De An.* V, c. 3; VII, 6-7. Averroes, *In II De An.* comm. 21, 32; III, comm. 4-6. Phil. Cancellarius, *De An.,* q. 10 (xvii). Guil. Alvernus, *De An.* V, 24. Joan. de Rupella, *De An.* I, 35-39. Alex. Halensis, *Summa* II, 1, p. 417. Albertus M., *Summa de Creat.* II, q. 4, a. 1, vol. 35, pp. 32-38; *Summa Theol.* II, tr. 13, q. 77, m. 1, vol. 33, p. 68.
[2] In such passages the editions (after that of Lyons 1569) generally have "But it must be said". The author, however, seems to be referring to an objection actually made by an objector in the disputation itself.

5   Furthermore, a form does not have being on account of matter, but matter has being on account of a form.[3] Hence the soul is not united to the body that the body may be perfected, but rather the body, if the soul is a form, is united to it for the soul's perfection. But the soul does not need the body for its own perfection, since it can exist and can understand apart from the body. Therefore, the soul is not united to the body as a form.

6   Furthermore, the union of form and matter is natural. But a soul's union with a body is not natural, but miraculous; for it is said in the book *De Spiritu et Anima*[4] [14, *PL* XL, 790]: "It was completely miraculous that things so diverse and so divided could have been mutually conjoined." Therefore, the soul is not united to the body as a form.

7   Furthermore, according to the Philosopher in the book *De Caelo* [II, 6, 288b 14], "Every weakening is contrary to nature." Hence whatever weakens a thing is not united to it naturally. But the soul is weakened through union with the body, both as far as existence is concerned, because the body weighs down the soul, as is said in the book *De Spiritu et Anima* [XIV; *passim*], and as far as activity is concerned, because the soul can not know itself save by withdrawing itself from all corporeal connections *(nexibus)*, as the same book says [XXXII]. Therefore the soul's union with the body is not natural; and so we come to the same conclusion as before.

8   Furthermore, the Commentator says on VIII *Metaphysica* [comm. 16] that when that which is in potency actually comes into being *(fit actu)*, this does not take place through anything additional. But when the soul is united to the body, something extrinsic is added to the body; because the soul is created by God and is infused into the body. Therefore the soul is not the act or the form of the body.

9   Furthermore, a form is derived from the potentiality of matter. But a spiritual substance cannot be derived from the potentiality of corporeal matter. Therefore a spiritual substance cannot be united to the body as a form.

10   Furthermore, the congruity of spirit to spirit is greater than the congruity of spirit to body. But a spirit cannot be the form of another spirit. Therefore neither can a spiritual substance be the form of the body.

11   Furthermore, Augustine says that a soul and an angel are "like in nature and unlike in function" [*De Libero Arbitrio* III, 11, 32]. But an angel cannot be the form of the body; therefore neither can the soul.

12   Furthermore, Boethius says in his book *De Duabus Naturis* [I, *PL* LXIV, 1342]: "Nature is the specific difference that informs each thing."

---

[3] This saying, so often quoted by St. Thomas, originated with Averroes (*In II Physica*, comm. 26; 91).
[4] Cf. Art. 3, ad 6.

But the specific difference of an angel and of a soul is the same; namely, "rational". Therefore the nature of both is the same; and so we come to the same conclusion as before.

13 Furthermore, the soul is related to the whole and to the parts in the same way, because it is wholly in the whole body and wholly in every single part. But a spiritual substance, which the intellect is, "is not an act of any part of the body,"[5] as is said in III *De Anima* [II, 1, 413a 7]. Therefore, a spiritual substance is not the form of the whole body.

14 Furthermore, a natural form existing in the body does not act outside the body. But the soul existing in the body acts outside the body, for in the Council of Ancyra[6] it is said of women who think they go to Diana by night that what they think they suffer in body occurs to them in spirit, and so also their spirit acts outside the body. Therefore, a spiritual substance is not united to the body as its natural form.

15 Furthermore, in the book *De Articulis Fidei* [I, 4, of Alan of Lille] it is said: "Neither form without matter nor matter without form is a subject." But the body is the subject of some accidents; therefore the body is not matter without form. If, then, a spiritual substance accrues to it as form, it would follow that there will be two forms in one and the same thing, which is impossible.

16 Furthermore, the corruptible and the incorruptible differ in genus, nor is anything said of them univocally, as the Philosopher and his Commentator make clear in X *Metaphysica* [10, 1058b 28]. Therefore, the corruptible and the incorruptible differ more widely than do two contraries which are species of one genus. But Boethius says [*In Categorias* IV, *PL* LXIV, 282] that one of two contraries does not aid the other toward actual being. Therefore, a spiritual substance, since it is incorruptible, does not aid the corruptible body toward actual being; and hence is not its form, since a form gives actual being to matter.

17 Furthermore, whatever is united to another through something which is not of its own essence is not united to it as a form. But the intellect is united to the body through the imagination, which does not belong to the substance of the intellect, as the Commentator says on III *De Anima* [comm. 5; 36]. Therefore the spiritual substance which is the intellect is not united to the body as a form.

18 Furthermore, every spiritual substance is intellectual. Now every intellectual substance is set apart from matter, since it is something intel-

---

5 This quotation is frequently cited by the Scholastic philosophers and is constantly referred to III *De An.;* where, however, it is not to be found, except implicitly in c. 4.
6 The document in question is to be found in the *Decreta Gratiani* (c. 12, C. 26 a. 5, vol. I, p. 1030), Richter-Friedburg, Leipzig, 1879. There the reference is to the *concilium Anquirense* or *Ancyrense.*

lectual through its freedom from matter. Therefore no spiritual substance is a form in matter, and so it cannot be united to the body as a form.

19 Furthermore, out of matter and form a single thing comes into being. If, then, a spiritual substance is united to the body as a form, out of the spiritual substance and the body one single thing should come into being. The intelligible forms which are received in the intellect will be received in corporeal matter; which is impossible, because forms received in corporeal matter are intelligible only in potency. Therefore the substance is not united to the body as a form.

But on the other hand there is what Dionysius says in the fourth chapter of *De Divinis Nominibus* [lec. 1], that the soul is an intellectual substance which has unfailing life. But the soul is the form of the body, as is clear from the definition of it set down in II *De Anima* [1, 412b 5]. Therefore some spiritual or intellectual substance is united to the body as a form.

ANSWER. It must be said that the difficulty of this question arises from the fact that a spiritual substance is a kind of self-subsistent thing. Now a form must have actual being in something else, that is, in matter, of which it is the act and the perfection. Hence it seems to be contrary to the character of a spiritual substance that it should be the form of the body. And for this reason Gregory of Nyssa[7] in his book *De Anima* [*PG* XLV, 199] accused Aristotle of asserting that the soul is not self-subsistent, and that it is corrupted when the body is corrupted, because he asserted it as the entelechy, that is, as the act or perfection, of the physical body.

But yet, if one carefully studies the matter, it becomes clearly evident that some substance must be the form of the human body. For it is obvious that understanding belongs to "this particular man" (as, for instance, Socrates or Plato). Now no activity belongs to any given thing except through some form which exists in the thing itself, either a substantial or an accidental form, because nothing acts or functions except in consequence of its being actual. Now each individual thing is actual through some form, either substantial or accidental, since a form is an act; thus, for instance, fire is actually fire through "fireness", and actually hot through heat. Accordingly, it must be the case that the principle of that activity which is understanding should be in "this man" in the way of a form. Now the principle of this activity is not a form whose actual being is dependent on matter and tied down to or immersed in matter, because this activity is not effected by means of the body, as is proven in III *De Anima* [4, 429a 24]; and hence the principle of this activity possesses

---

[7] Cc. 2-3 of Nemesius Emesenus' work *De Natura Hominis*, which deal with the soul, were in circulation in the Middle Ages under the name of Gregory of Nyssa, and were printed also among Gregory's writings by Migne (*PG* XLV).

an activity that has nothing in common with corporeal matter. Now, the way in which each thing acts is a consequence of its being. Hence the actual being of that principle must be an actual being which is raised above corporeal matter and not dependent on it. Now this is characteristic of a spiritual substance. It is necessary to say, therefore, if the preceding considerations are put together, that some kind of substance is the form of the human body.

But there are some who, while admitting that understanding is the act of a spiritual substance, have denied that such a spiritual substance is united to the body as a form. Among these Averroes asserted that the possible intellect, in its actual being, is separated from the body. He saw nevertheless that unless there were some union of it with "this man", its act could not pertain to "this man". For if there are two substances entirely unconnected, when one is acting or functioning, the other is not said to be functioning. And hence he asserted that such an intellect, which he said was entirely separated from the body in its actual being, is connected with "this man" through phantasms, for this reason, that the intelligible species, which is a perfection of the possible intellect, is based on the phantasms from which it is abstracted.[8] So, therefore, it has a two-fold kind of actual being: one in the possible intellect, of which it is the form, and the other in the phantasms from which it is abstracted. Now the phantasms are in "this man" because the imaginative power is a power within the body; that is, one which has a corporeal organ. The intelligible species itself, therefore, is the medium which joins the possible intellect to "the individual man".

But this connection is in no way sufficient to explain the fact that "this individual man" understands. For, as Aristotle says in his book III *De Anima* [7, 431a 14], the phantasms are related to the possible intellect as color is to the sight.[9] Accordingly, the intelligible species abstracted from the phantasms is in the possible intellect in the same way as the species "color" is in the sense of sight. Now the intelligible species is in the phantasms in the same way as a species which makes seeing possible *(species visibilis)* is in the physical object which is a wall. Now owing to the fact that the species which makes seeing possible, the form "sight", is based on the color of the wall, the act of seeing is not connected with the wall as with a seeing object, but as with a seen object: for by

---

[8] In almost the same formulas this obscure opinion of Averroes on the intellect's connection with man is elsewhere succinctly expressed; cf. *Summa Theol.* I, q. 76, a. 1, resp.; *Q. De An.* 2; *De Unit. Intell.*, c. 3, §63. "This connection," says Scotus *In IV Sent.*, d. 43, q. 2, 5), "neither himself (the Commentator) nor any of his followers could explain, nor could he by that connection save the thesis that man understands."

[9] Cf. *Q. De An.*, 2, resp.: "as sensible things to the sense and colors to the sight", for the Philosopher says οἶον αἰσθήματα; but the expression "as colors to the sight" has been taken from 430a 15, where it is used of the agent intellect.

means of it the wall does not see, but is seen; for what constitutes a knower is not the fact that there is in him a form whose image is in some knowing power, but the fact that there is in him the cognitive power itself. And "this man," accordingly, will not be one who understands because of the fact that in him are phantasms whose image, which is an intelligible species, is in the possible intellect; but it does follow because of this fact that his phantasms are understood by him.[10] But the possible intellect itself, which is the understanding power, must be in "this man" in the way of a form, precisely in order that "this man" may understand. He seems to have made a mistake also in regard to the character of connection itself, since the intelligible species is not one with the possible intellect, save insofar as it has been abstracted from the phantasms: for only so is it understood in act, whereas insofar as it is in the phantasms it is understood only in potency.[11] By this fact, then, is proved rather the disconnection of the possible intellect from the phantasms than its connection with them, for it must be the case that two things are entirely disconnected when something cannot be united to one of them unless it has been previously separated from the other.

Setting aside this view then as impossible, we must consider that Plato produced a better result by asserting that "this man" understands, and yet that a spiritual substance is not united to the body as a form. For, as Gregory of Nyssa[12] tells us [*De An. PG* XLV, 216], Plato asserted that the intellectual substance which is called the soul is united to the body by a kind of spiritual contact: and this is understood in the sense in which a thing that moves or acts touches the thing that is moved or is passive, even though it be incorporeal; and for this reason Aristotle says in I *De Generatione* [6, 323a 28] that certain things touch and yet are not touched, because they act and are not passive. And hence Plato used to say, as the aforesaid Gregory relates, that man is not something that is composed of soul and body, but is a soul using a body, so that he is understood to be in a body in somewhat the same way as a sailor is in a ship; and Aristotle seems to be touching upon this in II *De Anima* [1, 413a 8]. Thus, then, "this man" also understands, inasmuch as "this man" is the very spiritual substance which is the soul, whose proper act is understand-

---

[10] "Aliarum intellecta" ("things understood of other . . ."), as found in the manuscripts, cannot be let stand. The sense is clear from the parallel passage in *De Unit. Intell.* c. 3, §66: "From this it would follow that man would not understand, but that his phantasms would be understood by the possible intellect."

[11] As he says in *De Unit. Intell.,* c. 3, §65, the species in the phantasm and in the intellect cannot effect the connection of these, because the species is not numerically the same in both. This argument of Aquinas is unacceptable to Aegidius Romanus (*De Pluralitate Intellectus*), because he thinks the species is the same, but that it exists in both in a different way.

[12] The text of Nemesius Emesenus is given in *De Unit. Intell.* (c. 3, §76): Plato "does not mean that man is made up of body and soul, but that he is a soul using a body and, as it were, clothed with a body."

ing, even though, nevertheless, this substance does not exist as the form of the body.

But for the invalidation of this argument the one point suffices which Aristotle brings forward directly against this position in II *De Anima* [1, 412a]. For if the soul were not united to the body as a form, it would follow that the body and its parts would not have specific actual being through the soul; and this is seen to be obviously false: because once the soul departs, one does not say eye or flesh or bone, save equivocally, as one says painted eye or eye of stone. And hence it is obvious that the soul is the form and "the essence of this body", that is, that from which this body has the character of its own species. Exactly how this can be, however, we must proceed to investigate.

Now it must be borne in mind that the more perfect a form is, the more does it surpass corporeal matter. This is clear from induction in regard to the various orders of forms. For the form of an element does not have any activity but the one which takes place through active and passive qualities, which are the dispositions of corporeal matter. But the form "mineral body" has an activity that goes beyond active and passive qualities, and is a consequence of its species by reason of the influence of a heavenly body; for instance, that a magnet attracts iron, and that a sapphire cures an abscess.[13] And further, the vegetative soul *(anima vegetabilis)* has an activity to which the active and passive organic qualities of course contribute; but nevertheless, over and above the power of qualities like these, the soul itself achieves an effect of its own by nurture and growth up to a definite limit, and by carrying on other functions of this sort. And the sensing soul *(anima sensitiva)* has a further activity to which the active and the passive qualities do not extend in any way, save insofar as they are needed for the composition of the organ through which this sort of activity is exercised; such as seeing, hearing, desiring, and the like.

But the most perfect of forms, the human soul, which is the end of all natural forms, has an activity that goes entirely beyond matter, and does not take place through a corporeal organ; namely, understanding. And because the actual being of a thing is proportioned to its activity, as has been said, since each thing acts according as it is a being *(ens)*, it must be the case that the actual being of the human soul surpasses corporeal matter, and is not totally included in it, but yet in some way is touched upon by it. Inasmuch, then, as it surpasses the actual being of corporeal matter, having of itself the power to subsist and to act, the human soul is a spiritual substance; but inasmuch as

---

[13] Cf. *De Unit. Intell.,* c. 1, §27: "just as the magnet has the power to attract iron, and the sapphire to stop bleeding."

it is touched upon by matter and shares its own actual being with matter, it is the form of the body. Now it is touched upon by corporeal matter for this reason, that the highest point of the lowest always touches the lowest point of the highest, as Dionysius makes clear in the seventh chapter [lec. 4] of *De Divinis Nominibus;* and consequently the human soul, which is the lowest in the order of spiritual substances, can communicate its own actual being to the human body, which is the highest in dignity, so that from the soul and the body, as from form and matter, a single being results. But if a spiritual substance were composed of matter and form, it would be impossible for it to be the body's form; because it is essential to matter that it be not in anything else, but that it should itself be the primary subject.

As to the first argument, therefore, it must be said that a spiritual substance, although it is not completely grasped by the body, is nevertheless in some way or other touched upon by it, as has been said.

As to the second, it must be said that understanding is an activity of the human soul, inasmuch as the soul goes beyond its relation to corporeal matter and consequently understanding does not come about through any corporeal organ. Yet we may say that the composite itself (that is, man) understands, inasmuch as the soul, which is its formal part, has this proper activity, just as the activity of any part is attributed to the whole; for a man sees with his eye, walks with his foot, and in like fashion understands through his soul.

As to the third, it must be said that the soul has subsistent actual being, inasmuch as its own actual being does not depend on the body, seeing that it is something raised above corporeal matter. And yet it receives the body into a share in this actual being in such a way that there is one actual being of soul and of body, which is the actual being of a man. Now if the body were united to it in consequence of another actual being, it would follow that this union was accidental.

As to the fourth, it must be said that the soul by its very essence, and not on the basis of something added, is the form of the body. Nevertheless, inasmuch as it is affected by the body, it is a form; but inasmuch as it goes beyond a relationship with the body, it is called a spirit or a spiritual substance.

As to the fifth, it must be said that no part has the perfection of a nature, when separated from the whole. And hence the soul, since it is a part of a human nature, does not have the perfection of its own nature, save in union with the body. This is clear from the following fact: the soul itself has such virtuality that certain powers which are not acts of corporeal organs flow from it, inasmuch as it goes beyond its relationship with the body; and again, that powers which are acts of the organs flow from it, inasmuch as it can be dependent on corporeal

[37]

matter. Nor is a thing perfect in its own nature unless what is virtually contained in it can be actually brought out. And hence the soul, although it can exist and can understand when separated from the body, nevertheless does not have the perfection of its own nature when it is separated from the body, as Augustine says in XII *Super Genesi ad Litteram* [35, 68].

As to the sixth, it must be said that "miracle" is not to be taken in that passage in the sense of something opposed to natural activity, but in the sense in which even natural works themselves are called miracles, seeing that they proceed from the incomprehensible power of God. And in this sense Augustine says in *Super Joannem* [24, 1], that the fact that God produces from a few seeds as great a number of sheaves of grain as is sufficient to feed the whole human race is more marvelous than that He fed five thousand men with five loaves of bread.

As to the seventh, it must be said that that through which a thing is weakened, once its nature has been presupposed, is not something natural. Nevertheless it frequently happens that there is something which pertains to the nature of a thing, in consequence of which there nevertheless follows some weakness or defect in that thing: thus, for instance, to be composed of contraries is something natural to an animal, and in consequence of this death and corruption follow in it. And similarly it is something natural for the soul to need phantasms for understanding, and yet in consequence of this it follows that the soul, in its understanding, is made less than higher substances. As for the statement that the soul is weighed down by the body, this is not a consequence of the body's nature, but of its corruption, according to that passage in *Wisdom* IX [15]: "The body which is corrupted is a load upon the soul." But as for the statement that the soul withdraws itself from corporeal connections in order to understand itself, this must be understood as meaning that it abstracts itself from them as it abstracts from objects, because the soul is understood through the negation of all corporeity.[14] Yet the soul is not withdrawn from them in its actual being; nay, rather, if certain corporeal organs have been harmed, the soul cannot directly understand either itself or anything else, as when the brain is injured.

As to the eighth, it must be said that the higher a form is, the more does it need to be produced by a more powerful agent. Hence, since the human soul is the highest of all forms, it is produced by the most powerful agent, namely, God; yet in a way quite different from the

---

[14] This is certainly the Aristotelian explanation of the "flight from sensible things," but it does not reproduce the full meaning of such statements in the works of the Platonists.

way in which other forms are produced by any agents whatever. For the other forms are not subsistent: and hence they do not possess actual being, but some things have being through them; and hence their coming into being is due to the fact that some matter or subject is brought from potency into act: and this is a bringing forth of the form from the potency of matter, without the addition of anything extrinsic. But the soul itself has subsistent actual being; and hence coming into being is strictly due to it, and the body is brought over to its actual being. And on this account it is said that the soul exists from the outside and that it is not brought forth from the potency of matter. And hence the solution to the ninth argument is clear.

As to the tenth, it must be said that spirit fits in with spirit rather than with body by a congruity of nature. But by a congruity of relationship which is required between form and matter, spirit fits in with body more than spirit does with spirit: since two spirits are two acts, whereas the body is related to the soul as potency is to act.

As to the eleventh, it must be said that the angel and the soul are alike in their generic nature, inasmuch as both are intellectual substances. But the angel is superior in its specific nature, as Dionysius makes clear in the fourth chapter of *De Caelesti Hierarchia* [§2].

As to the twelfth, it must be said that "rational", understood in the strict sense, is the difference of "soul", not of "angel", but rather "intellectual", as Dionysius uses the term; because an angel does not know truth through discursive reasoning *(discursum rationis)*, but through simple insight, which is understanding in the strict sense. Nevertheless, if "rational" be taken in a wide sense, then it must be said that it is not the ultimate specific difference, but is divided into other specific differences because of the different degrees of understanding.

As to the thirteenth, it must be said that the intellect is not said to be the act of any part of the body, inasmuch as it is a power that does not make use of an organ. Nevertheless the soul's very substance is united to the body as a form, as has been said.

As to the fourteenth, it must be said that with reference to those women the running about *(discursus)* is said to take place in the spirit, not that the spirit (that is, the substance of the soul) functions outside the body, but because visions of this sort are formed in the spirit; that is, in the soul's imagination *(in phantastico animae)*.

As to the fifteenth, it must be said that matter without form, strictly speaking, cannot be a subject, seeing that "subject" is, strictly speaking, used of something that is actual being; but "living body" receives the character of actual being, so as to be able to be a subject, from no other form than the soul, as will be demonstrated below (Art. III).

[39]

As to the sixteenth, it must be said that "corruptible" and "incorruptible" do not belong to the same genus, from the standpoint of natural philosophy, because of the different mode of actual being and the different character of potency in each; although they may belong to the same logical genus, which is understood on a basis of their intelligible concept alone. Now the soul, although it is incorruptible, is nevertheless in no other genus than the body because, since it is a part of a human nature, to be in a genus or in a species or to be a person or hypostasis is not characteristic of the soul, but of the composite. And hence, also, it cannot be called "this something", if by this phrase is meant an hypostasis or person, or an individual situated in a genus or in a species. But if "this something" means every thing which is able to be self-subsistent, in this sense the soul is "this something."

As to the seventeenth, it must be said that that statement of the Commentator is impossible, as has been pointed out.

As to the eighteenth, it must be said that it is essential to intellectual substance that it be free from matter on which its being would depend as something totally tied down by matter. And hence nothing prevents the soul from being an intellectual substance and the form of the body, as has been said above.

As to the nineteenth, it must be said that out of a human soul and body a single thing comes into being in such a way that the soul nevertheless surpasses its relationship to the body; and because of that part by which it surpasses the body, intellectual power is attributed to it. And hence the intelligible species which are in the intellect need not be received in corporeal matter.

ARTICLE III

THE third question is: Is the spiritual substance, which is the human soul, united to the body through a medium?[1] No (?)

And it would seem that it is. *1* For Dionysius says in the thirteenth chapter of *De Caelesti Hierarchia* [§3] that the highest things are joined to the lowest through intermediates. But between a spiritual substance and a body there are intermediates, the vegetative soul and the sentient soul. Therefore the spiritual substance which is the rational soul is united to the body through the medium of the vegetative and the sentient souls.

2 Furthermore, the Philosopher says in II *De Anima* [1, 412b 5] that "it is the act of an organic body having life potentially." The physical organic body, therefore, having life potentially, is related to the soul as matter is to form. But this latter, namely, the physical organic body, does not exist except through some substantial form. Therefore that substantial form, whatever it may be, is present in matter before the spiritual substance which is the rational soul, and so for the same reason are the other subsequent forms, which are the sentient and the vegetative souls.

3 Furthermore, although matter is not a genus and form is not a difference, because neither of these is predicated of the composite whereas genus and difference are predicated of the species; nevertheless, according to the Philosopher in VIII *Metaphysica* [2, 1043a 19; 3, 1043b 30] the genus is derived from the matter and the difference from the form. But the genus of man is "animal", which is derived from a sentient nature, whereas the difference is "rational", which is derived from the rational soul. Therefore the sentient nature is related to the rational soul as matter is to form. But the sentient nature is perfected by the sentient soul. Therefore the sentient soul exists in nature before the rational soul, and for the same reason so do all the other previous forms.

4 Furthermore, as is proven in VIII *Physica* [4, 254b 22], every self-moving thing is divided into two parts, of which one is the mover and the other the object moved. But man and any animal whatever is a self-moving thing; now the motor part of it is the soul, and the

---

[1] *De Natura Materiae,* cc. 8-9 (a work that is probably genuine) ; *Contra Gentiles* II, cap. 71; *Summa Theol.**, I, q. 76, a. 3, 4, 6, 7; *Q. De Anima** 9; *In II De An.,* lec. 1, 234; *In VIII Met.* lec. 5; *Quodl.* I, a. 6; XII, a. 9; *Compend. theol.,* 91-92; (The question is not taken up in *Comment. in Sent.,* and is scarcely raised in *Contra Gentiles;* later it was his custom to treat it in detail.)

Avicenna, *Liber De Sufficientia* 1, c. 2 (on the form of corporeity) Isaac de Stella, *Epistola De Anima,* PL 194, 1881. Alcherus de Claravalle, *De Spiritu et Anima* PL XL, 780, c. 14 and elsewhere. Phil. Cancellarius, *De An.,* q. 10b (xvii). Guil. Alvernus, *De An.* VI, 35-36 (indirectly). Ioan. de Rupella, *De An.* I, 35-37. Alex. Halensis, *Summa* II, 1, p. 419 sqq. *Summa Philos.,* tr. 4, c. 13 (and elsewhere, teaching the plurality of forms). Roger Bacon, *Comm. Nat.* IV, 3, c. 4. Albertus M., *Summa Theol.* II, tr. 13, q. 77, m. 1, vol. 33 p. 68.

moved part cannot be mere matter but must be a body, because every thing that is moved is a body, as is proven in VI *Physica* [4 and 10]. Now a body exists through some form. Therefore some form exists in matter previous to the soul; and so we come to the same conclusion as before.

5 Furthermore, Damascene says [*De Fide Orth.* III, 6, *PG*, XCIV, 1006] that so great is the simplicity of the Divine Essence, that it is not fitting for the Word to be united to the flesh except through the medium of a soul. Therefore a difference based on "simple" and "composite" prevents some things from being able to be conjoined without a medium. But the rational soul and the body differ very widely on a basis of "simple" and "composite." Therefore, it must be the case that they are united through a medium.

6 Furthermore, St. Augustine says in his book *De Spiritu et Anima* [XIV, *PL* XL, 789] that "the soul which is truly a spirit and the flesh which is truly a body are easily and conveniently conjoined in their extremities, that is, in the soul's imagination *(in phantastico animae)*, which is not a body but is like a body, and in the body's sense-appetite *(sensualitate)*, which is almost a spirit, because it cannot come into being without the soul." The soul, then, is conjoined to the body through two media, namely, the imagination and the sense-appetite.

7 Furthermore, in the same book [XV] it is said: "Although the soul is incorporeal, it manages the body through the more subtle part of the nature of its body, that is, through fire and air." [2] Now the soul manages the body in the same way in which it is united to it; for when the elements through which the soul manages the body are lacking, the soul departs from the body, as Augustine says in VII *Super Genesi ad Litteram* [19]. Therefore the soul is united to the body through a medium.

8 Furthermore, things which differ most widely are not conjoined unless through a medium. But the corruptible and the incorruptible differ most widely, as is said in X *Metaphysica* [10, 1058b 28]. Therefore the human soul, which is incorruptible, is not united to the corruptible body except through a medium.

9 Furthermore, a certain philosopher[3] says in the book *De Differentia Spiritus et Animae* that the soul is united to the body through the medium of a spirit. Therefore it is united to it through a medium.

---

2 This is found almost word for word in Augustine also (*De Gen. ad Litt.* III, 5, 7; VII, 19, 25).

3 Costa ben Luca, whose work was translated in the twelfth century by John of Spain, and was lectured on in the faculty of arts of the University of Paris. C. S. Baruch has published some selections (*Bibliotheca philos. mediae aetatis*, Innsbruck, 1878).

[42]

What "medicine"? would it need to be an intermediate class existence neither "form" nor "matter"?

10 Furthermore, those things which are essentially different are not united without a medium. For there must be something which makes these one, as is clear from VIII *Metaphysica* [6, 1045a]. But the soul and the body are essentially different. Therefore they cannot be united except through a medium.

11 Furthermore, the soul is united to the body in order that it may be perfected by a union of this sort, because the form does not exist for matter, but matter for form. Now the soul is perfected in consequence of its union with the body, especially as regards understanding through phantasms, namely, insofar as it understands by abstracting from phantasms. Therefore it is united to the body through phantasms, which are neither of the essence of the body nor of the essence of the soul. Therefore the soul is united to the body through a medium.

12 Furthermore, before the coming of the rational soul the body in the womb of the mother has some form. Now when the rational *Aristotle* soul comes, it cannot be said that this form disappears, because it does not lapse into nothingness, nor would it be possible to specify anything into which it might return. Therefore some form exists in the matter previous to the rational soul. ← *make human (abortion issue)?*

13 Furthermore, in the embryo before the coming of the rational soul, vital functions are manifest, as is clear from XVI *De Animalibus* [*De Generatione Animalium* II, 3, 736b 12]. But vital functions come *Aristotle* only from the soul. Therefore another soul exists in the body before the coming of the rational soul; and thus it seems that the rational soul is united to the body through the medium of another soul.

14 Furthermore, since "abstraction is not falsification," as is said in II *Physica* [2, 193b 35], the body about which mathematicians speak must have some sort of actual being. Since, therefore, it is not separated from sensible things, it follows that it is in the sensible things. But for the very being of a body there is needed a form of corporeity. Therefore the form of corporeity, at least, is presupposed in the human body, which is a sensible body, prior to the human soul.[4]

15 Furthermore, in VII *Metaphysica* [11, 1036a 26] it is said that every definition has parts, and that the parts of a definition are forms. In anything that is defined, therefore, there must be several forms. Since, therefore, man is a kind of defined thing, it is necessary to posit in him several forms; and so some form exists before the rational soul.

16 Furthermore, nothing imparts what it does not possess. But the rational soul does not possess corporeity, since it is incorporeal; therefore it does not impart corporeity to man, and so man must have this from another form. — *everything — even matter from form?*

---

[4] Here he seems to be referring to Avicenna, *Liber Sufficientiae* I, c. 2, where it is proved that there is a form of corporeity.

[43]

17 Furthermore, the Commentator says [*In I Met.*, comm. 17] that prime matter receives universal forms before particular ones; thus, it receives the form "body" before the form "animate body", and so forth. Since, therefore, the human soul is the ultimate form and the most specific one, it seems that it presupposes other universal forms in matter.

18 Furthermore, the Commentator says in his book *De Substantia Orbis* [I] that dimensions exist in matter before the elementary forms. But dimensions are accidents,[5] and presuppose some substantial form in matter; otherwise accidental actual being would be prior to substantial actual being. Therefore, prior to the form of a simple element there exists beforehand in matter some other substantial form; hence, for all the greater reason, prior to the rational soul.

19 Furthermore, according to the Philosopher in his book *De Generatione* [II, 4, 331a], air is more easily converted into fire than water is because of the fact that it agrees with fire in one quality, namely, heat. When, therefore, fire comes into being out of air, it is necessary that the heat remain specifically the same: because if the heat of fire and the heat of air were specifically different, there would be eight primary qualities and not four only; for the same reasoning would apply to the other qualities, every one of which is found in two elements. If, therefore, one were to say that it remains specifically the same but numerically different,[6] the conversion of air into fire will not be easier than that of water into fire, because the form of fire will have to break up two qualities in the air just as it does in water. The only remaining alternative, therefore, is that the heat is numerically the same. But this cannot be unless there is already in existence some substantial form, which remains one in both and preserves the subject of heat as one; for an accident cannot be numerically one unless its subject is already one. One must therefore say that prior to the form of a simple body, some substantial form is presupposed in matter; much more so, then, prior to the rational soul.

20 Furthermore, prime matter considered simply in itself is quite indifferent to all forms. If, then, certain forms and dispositions, through which prime matter is specialized to this or to that particular form, do not exist before others, this particular form will not be received in prime matter in preference to another particular form.

---

[5] Dimensions, namely, indeterminate dimensions, which St. Thomas defends in several places (v. g., *In IV Sent.*, d. 12, q. 1, a. 2, sol. 4; *In Boeth. De Trin.*, q. 4, a. 2; *Contra Gentiles* IV, cap. 81, etc.), but in the (genuine?) work *De Natura Materiae* (c. 4), he refutes them with many arguments, nor does he subscribe to them in his later works.

[6] Namely, in air the hot and the moist, in water the cold and the moist. This whole difficulty is discussed at length in *De Natura Materiae* (cc. 8-9).

21 Furthermore, matter is united to form through the potency whereby it is able to underlie form. But that potency is not the same as the essence of matter: for in that case matter would be exactly as simple as God, Who is His own potency. Some medium, therefore, comes in between matter and the soul and any other form.

But on the other hand, *i* there is this passage in the book *De Ecclesiasticis Dogmatibus* [XV, *PL* XLII, 1216]: "Neither do we say that there are two souls in man, . . . one, an animal soul, which gives life to the body, . . . the other, a spiritual soul, which subserves reason." From this we argue as follows: just as man belongs to the genus "animal", so he belongs to the genus "animate body", and "body", and "substance". But through that one and the same form which is the soul, he is both man and animal, as is clear from the passage quoted above. By the same reasoning, therefore, through that one and the same form he is given a place in all the higher genera; and thus there does not exist any form in matter prior to the soul.

ii Furthermore, God and the soul differ more widely than do soul and body. But in the mystery of the Incarnation, the Word was united to the soul immediately. Therefore, for all the greater reason can the soul be immediately united to the body.

iii Furthermore, what is intermediate must have something in common with both of the extremes. But there cannot be anything which is partly corporeal and partly spiritual. Therefore, there cannot be any medium between soul and body.

iv Furthermore, the Master says in his first distinction [*PL*, CLXXXXII, 655] of II *Sententiae* that the union of the soul with the body is an illustration of that blessed union whereby the beatified soul is conjoined with God. But that conjunction takes place without any medium. Therefore the former union does also.

v Furthermore, the Philosopher says in I *De Anima* [6, 411b 7] that the body does not hold the soul together, but rather the soul holds the body together; and in the same place the Commentator says [comm. 90, 91] that the soul is the cause of the body's continuity. But the body's continuity depends on the substantial form whereby the body is a body. Therefore the rational soul itself is the form in man whereby the body is a body.

vi Furthermore, the rational soul is more efficacious and more powerful than is the form of a simple element. But from the form of a simple element a simple body possesses whatever it substantially is. Therefore, for all the greater reason does the human body have from the soul whatever it substantially is; and so there does not exist beforehand any form or any medium.

[45]

ANSWER. [It must be said that the truth of this question depends to some extent on the preceding one. For if the rational soul is united to the body only through virtual contact, like a mover, as some have asserted, nothing would prevent us from saying that there are many intermediates between the soul and the body, and more so between the soul and prime matter. But if it be asserted that the soul is united to the body as a form, it must be said that it is united to the body immediately. For every form, whether substantial or accidental, is united to matter or to a subject. For each individual thing is one on the same basis on which it is a being.] Now, each individual thing is actually a being through a form, whether in the case of actual substantial being or in the case of actual accidental being. And hence every form is an act, and as a consequence it is the reason for the unity whereby a given thing is one. Therefore, just as we cannot say that there is any other medium whereby matter has actual being through its own form, so it cannot be said that there is any other medium uniting a form to matter or to a subject. In consequence of the fact that the soul, then, is the form of the body, there cannot be any medium between the soul and the body. But in consequence of the fact that it is a mover, from this point of view nothing prevents our asserting many media there: for obviously the soul moves the other members of the body through the heart, and also moves the body through the spirit.[7]

But then there is still a doubt about what is the proper subject of the soul, which is related to it as matter is to form. For on this point there are two opinions. For some say that there are many substantial forms in the same individual, and that one of these is the substrate of another; and on this view prime matter is not the immediate subject of the ultimate substantial form, but underlies it, with intermediate forms acting as media, so that matter itself, viewed as subject of a form, is the proximate subject of the second form; and so on down to the ultimate form. Thus, then, the proximate subject of the rational soul is the body perfected by the sentient soul, and to this latter is united the rational soul as a form. The other opinion is that in one individual there is but one substantial form; and on this view it is necessary to say that through the substantial form, which is the human soul, this individual has not only "being man", but "being animal", and "being alive", and "being body", and "substance", and "being." And thus in this particular man

---

[7] Cf. *Q. De An.* (9, ad 13): "It must be said that the heart is the primary instrument by means of which the soul moves the other parts of the body; and therefore through it as a medium the soul is united to the other parts of the body as the mover"; *ibid.,* ad 7: "although the same effect is partly produced by the dissolution, caused by the blood, of those humors whereby the heart is dilated and contracted." Perhaps then our text ought to read: "and also moves the heart through the spirit."

no other substantial form is prior to the human soul, and consequently neither is any accidental form; because in that case one would have to say that prime matter is first perfected through an accidental form rather than through the substantial form, which is impossible: for every accident must be grounded on some substance.

Now the diversity of these two opinions proceeds from the fact that some, in order to investigate the truths of nature, have taken as their starting point intelligible essences, and this was characteristic of the Platonists; whereas some began with sensible things, and this was characteristic of the philosophy of Aristotle, as Simplicius says in his commentary *Super Praedicamenta* [Preface]. The Platonists envisaged a definite order of genera and species, and held that the higher can always be understood apart from the lower, as, for instance, "man" apart from "this man", and "animal" apart from "man", and so on. They thought also that whatever is abstract in the intellect is abstract in reality; otherwise it seemed to them that the abstracting intellect would be false or futile, if there were no abstract thing corresponding to it; and on this account they also believed that mathematical objects exist apart from sensible things, because they are understood apart from them.[8] Hence they asserted "man in the abstract" apart from "these men", and so on up to "being", and "one", and "good", which they asserted as the highest virtue of things. For they saw that the lower is always more particular than what is above it, and that the nature of the higher is participated by the lower; now, that which participates serves as the material element for that which is participated, and hence they asserted that among abstract things the more universal a thing is, the more it is something formal.

But some, starting out along the same road, asserted on the contrary that the more universal a form is, the more material it is. And this is the position of Avicebron in his book *Fons Vitae*[9]: he asserted a prime matter without any form which he called universal matter; and he said that it is common to spiritual and corporeal substances, and to it, he said, there is added a universal form which is the form of substance. Now, matter thus existing under the form of substance, he said, receives in a part of itself the form of corporeity, while another part of it which pertains to spiritual substances remains without a form of this sort. And so he proceeded to assert in matter one form under another according to the order of genera and species, down to the ulti-

---

[8] It may be the case that changes from the plural to the singular number, which are common to all our manuscripts, were in the autograph text itself, the author sometimes thinking of the Platonists, sometimes of Plato.
[9] Compare a similar exposition and refutation of Avicebron's doctrine in Art. I, ad 9. The repetition can be explained on the ground that St. Thomas here wishes to show the similarity between Avicebron's doctrine and that of the Platonists.

mate specific species. And this position, although it seems to disagree with the first, nevertheless in actual truth agrees with it and is a consequence of it. For the Platonists asserted that the more universal and the more formal a cause is, the more remote is its perfection in a given individual: and hence as an effect of the first abstract, that is, of the good, they put down prime matter,[10] in order to have a primary subject corresponding to the supreme agent; and so following, according to the order of abstract causes and forms that have a share in matter, just as a more universal abstract is more formal, so a more universal participated form is more material.

But this position, according to the true principles of philosophy which Aristotle considered, is an impossible one. In the first place, because no individual instance of substance would be "one" in an unqualified sense. For a thing that is one in an unqualified sense does not come into being from two acts, but from potency and act inasmuch as that which is in potency comes into being actually. And on this account "white man" is not one in an unqualified sense, but "two-footed animal" is one in an unqualified sense, because the very thing which is animal is two-footed. But if "animal" were something in isolation, and if "two-footed" were something in isolation, "man" would not be one but several, as the Philosopher argues in III and in VIII *Metaphysica* [4, 999b 25; 6, 1045a 16]. It is obvious, therefore, that if there were a manifold of many substantial forms in one individual instance of substance, the individual instance of substance would not be one in an unqualified sense, but in a qualified sense, like "white man."

Secondly, because the essential character of an accident consists in the fact that it is in a subject, yet in this sense, that by a subject is meant an actual being and not one merely in potency, and in this sense a substantial form is not in a subject but in matter. Whenever there is a form, therefore, of which some actual being is a substrate in any sense, that form is an accident. Now it is obvious that any substantial form, whatever it may be, makes a being actual and is a constituent thereof; and hence it follows that only the first form which comes to matter is substantial, whereas all those that come later are accidental.[11] And this is not ruled out by what some say, that the first form is in potency to the second form; because every subject is related to its own accident as potency is to act. Besides, a form of a body which would bestow capacity for life would be more complete than one which did

---

[10] Such is the doctrine of Proclus (*Instit. Theol.*, 72), but not of Plotinus, namely, that the most formal and universal cause, because its power has the widest range, produces the lowest and, as it were, the most distant effect in things; and this effect is matter.

[11] As he says in *Q. De. An.* 9, resp.: "between substantial form and matter, there cannot occur any intermediate substantial form."

not: and hence, if the form of a non-living body makes that body to be an actual subject, much more does the form of a body that has life in potency make that body to be an actual subject; and thus the soul would be a form in a subject, which is the essential characteristic of an accident.

Thirdly, because it would follow that in the acquiring of the last form, there would be generation not in an unqualified sense but in a qualified sense only. For since generation is a changing over from non-being into actual being, a thing is generated in an unqualified sense when it becomes a being, unqualifiedly speaking, from non-being in an unqualified sense. Now a thing which is already in existence as an actual being cannot become a being in an unqualified sense, but it can become "this particular being", as, for instance, "white being" or "large being", and this is becoming in a qualified sense. Since, then, it is the preceding form in matter which produces actual being, a subsequent form will not produce actual being in an unqualified sense, but "being this particular thing", as, for instance, "being man" or "being ass" or "being plant"; and so there will not be generation in an unqualified sense. And on this account, all the ancients who asserted that prime matter is actually something, such as fire or air or water or something in between, said that becoming was nothing but change;[12] and Aristotle solves their difficulty by asserting that matter exists only in potency, and he says that it is the subject of generation and corruption in an unqualified sense. And because matter is never denuded of all form, on this account whenever it receives one form it loses another, and vice versa.

Thus, therefore, we say that in "this man" there is no other substantial form than the rational soul, and that by it man is not only man, but animal, and living being, and body, and substance, and being. And this can be thought out in the following way. For the form is a likeness of the agent in the matter.[13] Now, in the case of active and functioning powers what we find is this, that the higher a power is, the more things does it include within itself, not in composite fashion but as a unit; thus, for instance, as a single power the common sense extends itself to all sense-objects, which the special senses apprehend as different powers. Now, it is characteristic of a more perfect agent to produce a more perfect form. And hence a more perfect form does by means of one thing all that lower forms do by means of different things, and still more: for example, if the form of non-living body confers on matter "actual being" and "being a body", the form of plant will confer on it this too, and "life" besides; and the sentient soul will confer

---

[12] This passage coincides almost verbatim with *Summa Theol.* I, q. 76, a. 4, resp.
[13] For an agent produces something that is like itself, and it acts by introducing a form.

[49]

this too and besides it will confer "sentient being"; and the rational soul will also confer this and besides it will confer "rational being". For this is the way in which the forms of natural things are found to differ in the order of increasing perfection, as is clear to anyone who looks at all the genera and species of natural things; and on this account the species are compared to numbers, as is said in VIII *Metaphysica* [3, 1043b 33], the species of which are made different through adding and subtracting one. And hence Aristotle also says in II *De Anima* [3, 414b 31]: "The vegetative is in the sentient," and *the sentient is in the intellectual*,[14] as "a triangle is in a quadrilateral" and a quadrilateral in a pentagon; for a pentagon virtually contains a quadrilateral: for it has this and still more; not that something proper to a quadrilateral and something proper to a pentagon exists outside the pentagon, as though there were two figures. So also the intellectual soul virtually contains the sentient soul, because it has this and still more, yet not in such a way that there are two souls. Now if we were to say that the intellectual soul differed essentially from the sentient soul in man, no reason could be given for the union of the intellectual soul with the body, since no activity proper to the intellectual soul takes place through a corporeal organ.

As to the first argument, therefore, it must be said that the quotation from Dionysius must be understood as referring to efficient causes, not to formal causes.

As to the second, it must be said that since the most perfect form imparts everything which the more imperfect forms impart and still more; matter, according as it is perfected by this form in the same kind of perfection wherein it is perfected by more imperfect forms, is considered as proper matter in relation to that kind of perfection which the more perfect form adds over and above the others; yet in such a way that this distinction among forms is not understood as something based on their essence, but only as something based on their intelligible concept. Thus, therefore, matter itself according as it is understood to be perfect in corporeal being capable of receiving life, is the proper subject of the soul.

As to the third, it must be said that since "animal" is that which is really "man", the distinction of animal nature from man is not based on a real diversity of forms as though there were one form whereby the being is animal, and another superadded form whereby it is man; but this distinction is based on intelligible concepts. For according as

---

[14] The reading of the manuscripts is certainly incorrect; cf. *Q. De An.* 2, obj. 3: "The Philosopher says in *De An.* II that just as a triangle is in a quadrilateral and a quadrilateral is in a pentagon, so the nutritive power is in the sentient, and the sentient is in the intellectual": and so in many other places to the same effect. The analogy is explained more fully in *De Unit. Intell.*, c. 1, §49.

the body is understood as perfected in sensible being by the soul, in this sense it is related to the ultimate perfection, which comes from the rational soul as such, as a material element is related to a formal element. For since genus and species signify certain conceptual entities, a real distinction of forms is not needed for the distinction between a species and a genus, but only a mental distinction.

As to the fourth, it must be said that the soul moves the body through knowledge and appetite. However, the sentient and the appetitive power in an animal have a definite organ, and thus the movement of the animal originates in that organ which is the heart, according to Aristotle [*De Gener. Anim.* II, 6, *et saepe*]. Thus, then, one part of the animal is what does the moving and the other is the part that is moved, so that the moving part may be taken to be the primary organ of the appetitive soul, and the remainder of the body is what is moved. But because in man the moving is done by the will and the intellect, which are not acts of any organ, the thing that does the moving will be the soul itself, considered on its intellectual side, whereas the moved thing will be the body, considered as something which is perfected by that soul in corporeal being.

As to the fifth, it must be said that in the Incarnation of the Word, the soul is set down as an intermediary between the Word and the flesh, not of necessity but because of fitness; and hence also, when the soul was separated from the body at the death of Christ, the Word remained immediately united to the flesh.

As to the sixth, it must be said that that book is not Augustine's,[15] nor is it very authentic, and in this quotation the language is rather inexact. For both things pertain to the soul, both the imagination and the sense-appetite: nevertheless, the sense-appetite is said to be connected with the flesh, insofar as it is an appetite for things pertaining to the body; whereas the imagination is said to be connected with the soul, insofar as in it there are likenesses of bodies apart from bodies. Now these are said to be intermediate between the soul and the flesh, not considering the soul as the form of the body, but considering it as the mover.

As to the seventh, it must be said that the management of the body pertains to the soul insofar as it is the mover, not insofar as it is the form. And although those things by which the soul manages the body are necessary for the soul's being in the body, as the proper dispositions of this sort of matter, nevertheless it does not follow from this that the

---

[15] Alcher of Clairvaux wrote it about 1165. Cf. below, Art. XI, ad 2; and *Q. De An.* 12, ad 1; "It must be said that the book *De Spiritu et Anima* is not Augustine's, but is said to have been that of a certain Cistercian; nor is much account to be taken of what is said in it."

character of the management and of the formal union is the same. For just as the soul, which is the mover and the form, is in substance the same soul, but is thought of as different, so also the things which are necessary for the formal union and for the management are the same things, although not considered from the same point of view.

As to the eighth, it must be said that the fact that the soul differs from the body as what is corruptible from what is incorruptible does not exclude its being the form of the body, as is clear from what was said above [Art. II, ad 16]; hence it follows that it is united immediately to the body.

As to the ninth, it must be said that the soul is said to be united to the body through the spirit, insofar as it is the mover, because that which is moved first by the soul in the body is the spirit, as Aristotle says in his book *De Causa Motus Animalium*[16] [X, 703a 10]; yet that book too is not very authoritative.

As to the tenth, it must be said that if any two things are essentially different in such a way that each has the complete nature of its own species, they cannot be united except through some binding and uniting medium. Now, the soul and the body are not of this sort, since they are both naturally a part of man, but they are related to each other as matter is to form, and their union is immediate, as has been shown.

As to the eleventh, it must be said that the soul is united to the body not merely in order to be perfected as regards understanding through phantasms, but also as regards its specific nature and as regards the other activities which it exercises through the body. Nevertheless, even granting that the soul is united to the body merely for the sake of understanding through phantasms, it would not follow that the union would take place through the medium of a phantasm: for the soul is united to the body for understanding in this sense, that through it man may understand; and this would not be the case if the union took place through phantasms, as was shown above.

As to the twelfth, it must be said that the body, before it receives a soul, has some form; however, that form does not remain when the soul comes. For the coming of the soul takes place through a kind of generation, and the generation of one thing does not occur without the corruption of the other; thus, for instance, when the form of fire is received in the matter of air, the form of air ceases to be in it actually and remains in potency only. Nor must it be said that the form comes into being or is corrupted, because coming into being and being corrupted are characteristics of that which has actual being, and actual being does not belong to a form as to something that exists, but as to that whereby

---

[16] περὶ ζῴων κινήσεως is generally regarded as spurious.

something is. And hence, too, nothing but the composite is said to come into being, insofar as it is brought from potency into act.

As to the thirteenth, it must be said that in the embryo certain vital functions are manifest. But some have said that such functions come from the soul of the mother; but this is impossible because it is an essential characteristic of vital functions that they come from an intrinsic principle which is the soul. On the other hand, some have said that from the outset the vegetative soul is present; and that same soul, when it is further perfected, becomes the sentient soul, and at length becomes the intellectual soul, but through the action of an outside agent which is God. But this is impossible: first, because it would follow that a substantial form is susceptible of degrees and that generation is a continuous movement; secondly, because it would follow that the rational soul is corruptible, so long as it is asserted that the foundation of the rational soul is a vegetative and sentient substance. Now it cannot be said that there are three souls in one man, as has been shown. The only thing left to say is that in the generation of man or of animal, there are many generations and corruptions succeeding one another reciprocally,[17] for when a more perfect form comes the less perfect form fades away. And thus, although in the embryo there is first the vegetative soul only, when it has attained a greater perfection the imperfect form is taken away, and the more perfect form takes its place, i.e., a soul which is vegetative and sentient simultaneously; and when the last departs there comes in the most complete ultimate form, which is the rational soul.

As to the fourteenth, it must be said that a mathematical body is called an abstract body; and hence, to say that a mathematical body exists in sensible things is to say two opposite things at the same time, as Aristotle argues in III *Metaphysica* [2, 998a 7] against certain Platonists who make this assertion. And yet it does not follow that abstraction is falsification, if a mathematical body exists in the intellect only: because the abstracting intellect does not think that some body exists which is not in sensible things, but it thinks that body by not thinking sensible objects; thus, for instance, if someone thinks "man", not thinking his risibility, he is not falsifying; but he would be falsifying if he thought "man is not a risible being." I say, nevertheless, that if "mathematical body" were in "sensible body", then since "mathematical body" has dimensions, it pertains only to the genus of quantity; hence no substantial form would be needed. But "body" which is in the genus of substance has a substantial form which is called "corporeity", which

---

[17] Roger Bacon attacks most bitterly this view of St. Thomas on the generation of man, which (he says) "theologians in England and all philosophers still" contradict (*Comm. Nat.* IV, 3, c. 1, p. 281 sqq.).

is not three dimensions, but is any substantial form whatever from which the three dimensions follow in matter, and this form in fire is "fireness", in the animal the sentient soul, and in man the intellectual soul.

As to the fifteenth, it must be said that the parts of a definition are formal or specific parts, not because of a real distinction between forms, but on the basis of a mental distinction, as has been said.

As to the sixteenth, it must be said that although the soul[18] does not have corporeity in act, yet it has it virtually, just as the sun has heat.

As to the seventeenth, it must be said that that order upon which the Commentator touches is a conceptual order only; because matter is understood to be perfected by a universal form before it is understood to be perfected by a special form, just as being is understood as something prior to living being, living being prior to animal, and animal prior to man.

As to the eighteenth, it must be said that any generic or specific actual being whatever is the thing of which the proper accidents of that genus or species are a consequence. And hence, when matter is already understood to be perfect in the genus which is "body", it is quite possible to understand therein dimensions, which are the proper accidents of this genus: and in this way the different elementary forms follow one after the other in matter, according to its different parts, in an intelligible order.

As to the nineteenth, it must be said that specifically the same heat is in fire and in air, because any quality is especially attributed to one element in which it exists perfectly, and is attributed concomitantly or derivatively to another element, yet in a more imperfect way. When, therefore, "fire" comes into being from "this air", the heat remains specifically the same, but it is augmented; nevertheless, it is not the same numerically,[19] because the same subject does not persist. Nor does this tend to create a difficulty as regards change, since the heat goes out of being in an accidental way, as a result of the subject's passing away, and not as a result of an opposite agent.

As to the twentieth, it must be said that matter, when looked at by itself, is related to all forms indifferently; but it is determined to special forms through the power of the mover, as is taught in II *De Generatione* [9, 335b], and corresponding to the intelligible order of forms in matter there is an order of natural agents. For among the

---

[18] This difficulty, which later writers made so much of, namely, that the soul, being simple and without quantity, cannot give matter quantity by informing it, does not trouble St. Thomas much. Everywhere he answers by saying that the higher form virtually contains that which the lower contains, by appealing to the example of numbers and figures.

[19] In *De Natura Materiae* (cc. 8-9) accidents are said to remain numerically the same, because the forms themselves are present "essentially, but not existentially."

celestial bodies themselves, one is more universally active than another: nor does the more universal agent act apart from inferior agents, but the ultimate proper agent acts in virtue of all the higher agents. And hence different forms are not implanted by different agents in one individual, but there is one form which is implanted by the proximate agent that virtually contains in itself all the preceding forms; and matter, inasmuch as it is considered to be perfected by the character of the more universal form and the consequent accidents, is specialized to the subsequent perfection.

As to the twenty-first, it must be said that although each genus is divided into potency and act, that potency itself which is in the genus of substance is matter, as form is act. And hence, matter does not exist under form through the medium of some other potency.

will + ∴ soul moves body directly

rational soul = most complete
ultimate form

Article IV

THE fourth question is: Is the whole soul in every part of the body?[1] *Yes, taken as a wholeness*

And it would seem that it is not. *1* For Aristotle[2] says in his book *De Causa Motus Animalium* [10, 703a 32]: "There is no need for the soul to be any one part of the body, but there is need for it to exist in some principle of the body." Now in nature nothing is in vain. Therefore the soul is not in every part of the body.

2 Furthermore, an animal is made up of body and soul. If, then, the soul were in every part of the body, every part of an animal would be an animal; which is incongruous.

3 Furthermore, in anything in which a subject is, the property of the subject also is. But all the powers of the soul are in the essence of the soul, just as properties are in a subject. Therefore, if the soul were in every part of the body, it would follow that all the powers of the soul were in every part of the body, and thus hearing will be in the eye and sight in the ear; which is incongruous.

4 Furthermore, no form which demands a dissimilarity of parts is found in every part; as is clear regarding the form "house", which is not in every part of a house but in the house as a whole. But forms which do not demand a dissimilarity of parts are in the individual parts, as, for instance, the form "fire" and the form "air". Now the soul is a form that demands a dissimilarity of parts, as is clear in the case of all animate things. Therefore the soul is not in every part of the body.

5 Furthermore, no form which is extended in correspondence with the extension of matter is entirely in every part of its matter. But the soul is extended in correspondence with the extension of matter; for it is said in the book *De Quantitate Animae* [V, 7]: I judge the soul to be as large "as the extent of the body allows it to be." Therefore the soul is not entirely in every part of the body.

6 Futhermore, that the soul is in every part of the body seems particularly apparent from the fact that it acts in every part of the body. But the soul acts where it is not; for Augustine says in his letter to Volusianus [*Epistola* CXXXVII, II, 5]: the soul feels and sees in the

---

[1] *In I Sent.*, d. 8, q. 5, a. 3; *Contra Gentiles* II, cap. 72; *Summa Theol.* I, q. 76, a. 8; *Q. de An.**, 10; *In De An.* I, lec. 14.

St. Augustine, *De Quant. Animae; De Immort. Animae* xvi; *De Trin.* VI, vi. Avicenna, *De An.* V, cc. 2-3. Alcherus de Claravalle, *De Spiritu et Anima*, 18-19. Phil. Cancellarius, q. 9 *De An.* Guil. Alvernus, *De An.* VI, 38-39. Ioan. de Rupella, *De An.* 1, 40. Albertus M., *Summa Theol.* II, tr. 13, q. 77, m. 4, vol. 33, p. 100. (There was no controversy on this matter, except as regards the way of expressing it, or further developments, for all approved of what Augustine had said).

[2] Cf. Art. III, n. 15. The whole passage is cited in *Q. De An.*, 10, obj. 4.

[56]

heavens, where it is not. It is not, therefore, necessary for the soul to be in every part of the body.

7 Furthermore, according to the Philosopher [*De An.* I, 3, 406b], when we move those things which are within us are moved. Now it may be the case that one part of the body is moved while another is at rest. If, therefore, the soul is in every part of the body, it follows that it is both in motion and at rest at the same time; which seems incongruous.

8 Furthermore, if the soul is in every part of the body, each part of the body will have an immediate relation to the soul, and thus the other parts will not depend on the heart. This is contrary to Jerome in his *Super Matthaeum* [XV, *PL* XXVI, 109] who says that "the most important thing in man is not in the brain, as Plato says, but in the heart, as Christ says."

9 Furthermore, no form which demands a definite shape can be where that shape is not. But the soul is in the body in connection with a definite shape; for the Commentator says on I *De Anima* [comm. 53, f. 119r] that every animal's body has its own proper shape, and this fact is evident in the case of the species: "for the lion's members do not differ from the stag's members except because of the difference of their souls." Therefore, since the shape of the whole is not found in a part, the soul will not be in a part. And this is what the same Commentator says on the same book [comm. 94, f. 126r], "that if the heart has a natural capacity for receiving a soul because it has a particular kind of shape, it is obvious that a part of it does not receive that soul, because a part does not have that particular shape."

10 Furthermore, the more abstract a thing is, so much the less is it limited to something corporeal. But an angel is more abstract than a soul. Now an angel is limited to some part of the movable object which it moves and is not in every part of it, as the Philosopher makes clear in IV *Physica* [VIII, 10, 267b 7], where he says that the mover of the heavens is not in the centre, but in a certain part of the circumference. Much less then is a soul in every part of its body.

11 Furthermore, if the soul's activity is in any particular part of the body, the soul itself is there. And by a parallel argument, in whatever part of the body there is the activity of the power of sight, there is the power of sight. But the activity of the power of sight would be in the foot, if the organ of the power of sight were there; hence the fact that the activity of sight is not there will be due merely to the absence of the organ. Accordingly, the power of sight will be there, if the soul is there.

12 Furthermore, if the soul is in every part of the body, it must be the case that wherever a given part of the body is, there is the soul.

[57]

But in the case of a growing child, parts begin to exist through growth, where they previously were not; therefore, his soul too begins to exist where it previously was not. But this seems impossible. For there are three ways in which a thing begins to exist where it previously was not: either through the fact that something quite new comes into being, as when the soul is created and is infused into the body; or through a changing over of the thing itself, as when the body is changed from place to place; or through the change of another thing into the thing itself, as when Christ's body begins to exist on the altar. And none of these can be said to happen in this case. Therefore the soul is not in every part of the body.

13 Furthermore, the soul is only in the body whose act it is. Now it is "the act of an organic body," as II *De Anima* [1, 412b 5] says. Since, then, not every part of the body is an organic body, it will not be in every part of the body.

14 Furthermore, there is a greater difference between the flesh and the bone of any one man than between the flesh of one man and the flesh of another. But one soul cannot be in two bodies of different men. Therefore it cannot be in all the parts of any one man.

15 Furthermore, if the soul is in every part of the body, it must be the case that if any part of the body is taken away, either the soul must be taken away: which is clearly false, since a man remains alive; or else it must be transferred from that part to other parts: which is impossible, since the soul is simple and consequently immovable. Therefore it is not in every part of the body.

16 Furthermore, nothing that is indivisible can be in anything but an indivisible object, since a place has to be commensurate with what is in that place. Now in the body it is possible to specify an indefinite number of indivisibles. If, then, the soul is in every part of the body, it will follow that it is in an indefinite number of places. And this cannot be, since it is of finite power.

17 Furthermore, since the soul is simple and without dimensional quantity, it seems that no wholeness can possibly be attributed to it save that of power. But it is not in every part of the body as regards its powers, in which the wholeness of its power is considered to be. Therefore the whole soul is not in every part of the body.

18 Furthermore, that a thing can be wholly in a whole and in all parts seems to be due to its simplicity. For in the case of bodies we see that this cannot happen. But the soul is not simple, but is composed of matter and form. Therefore it is not in every part of the body. Proof of the minor: the Philosopher in II *Metaphysica* [I, 8, 988b 24] censures those who assert that corporeal matter is the first principle, because "they asserted only the elements of bodies, but not of things that do

[58]

not have bodies." There is accordingly some incorporeal element too. But an element is a material principle. Therefore incorporeal substances also, such as an angel and a soul, have a principle too.

19 Furthermore, "certain animals live, even when cut in two".[3] Now it cannot be said that either of the two parts lives through the whole soul. Therefore even before the cutting, the whole soul was not in that part, but part of the soul was.

20 Furthermore, "whole" and "perfect" are identical, as is said in III *Physica* [6, 207a 13]. Now a thing is perfect "which attains its proper excellence", as is said in VI *Physica* [3, 246a 13]. Now the proper excellence of the human soul, as regards the intellect, is not an act of any part of the body. Therefore the soul is not entirely in every part of the body.

But on the other hand *i* there is what Augustine says in III *De Trinitate* [VI, 6, 8], that the soul "is wholly in the whole being and wholly in every part of it."

ii Furthermore, Damascene says [*De Fide Orth.* 1, 13, *PG* XCIV, 854A; II, 3, 870C] that an angel is where it acts; by a parallel argument, therefore, also the soul. But the soul acts in every part of the body, because every part of the body is nourished, grows, and is sentient. Therefore, the soul is in every part of the body.

iii Furthermore, the soul is of greater power than material forms. But material forms, such as fire or air, are in every part; much more so, the soul.

iv Furthermore, it is said in the book *De Spiritu et Anima* [XVIII, *PL* XL, 793] that "The soul by its presence vivifies the body." But every part of the body is vivified by the soul. Therefore the soul is present in every part of the body.

ANSWER.[4] It must be said that the truth of this question depends on the preceding ones. For it has previously been pointed out that the soul is united to the body not only as a mover, but as a form. And later on it was shown that a soul does not presuppose in matter other substantial forms, which would give substantial actual being to a body or to its parts; but that both the whole body and all its parts have actual substantial and specific being through the soul, and, when the soul departs, just as "man" or "animal" or "living body" does not remain, so neither "eye" nor "flesh" nor "bone" remain, except in an equivocal sense, like things painted or made of stone.[5] Thus, then, since every

---

[3] This statement is cited from *Met.* VII, c. 16, 1040b 13; but cf. rather I *De Anima*, c. 5, 411b as well as St. Thomas' commentary.
[4] The correspondence between this *responsio* and that given in *Q. De An.*, 10 is remarkable.
[5] Thus Aristotle, II, *De An.*, 1, 412b 21.

act is in that of which it is the act, it must be that the soul, which is the act of the whole body and of all the parts, is in the whole body and in every one of its parts. ✳ *in nurturing role, sentient soul*

But yet the whole body is related in one way to the soul and in another to its parts. For the soul is indeed the act of the whole body primarily and essentially, but of the parts in their relation to the whole. To make this clear it must be considered that, since matter is for the sake of form, the matter must be such as suits the form. In those things which are subject to corruption the more imperfect forms, which are of weaker power, have few activities, for which dissimilarity of parts is not required, as is clear in the case of all inanimate bodies. But the soul, since it is a form of higher and greater power, can be the principle of different activities, for the carrying out of which dissimilar parts of the body are required. And consequently every soul requires a diversity of organs in parts of the body of which it is the act; and all the greater diversity in proportion as the soul is more perfect. Thus, then, the lowest forms perfect their matter in a uniform way, but the soul does this in a non-uniform way, with the result that the entirety of the body of which the soul is primarily and essentially the act is made up of dissimilar parts.

But we still have to inquire into the statement: the soul is wholly in the whole and wholly in each individual part. To make this clear, we must consider that wholeness is primarily and more obviously something based on quantity, inasmuch as a whole is called a quantum, which is naturally susceptible of division into quantitative parts; and this sort of wholeness cannot be ascribed to forms except in an accidental sense, namely, insofar as they are accidentally divided by the division of a quantity, as whiteness is divided by the division of a surface. But this is characteristic of those forms only which are extended along with quantity; and the reason why this latter property belongs to some forms is that they have similar, or almost similar, matter in their whole and in a part. And hence forms which require great dissimilarity in the parts do not have this sort of extension and wholeness, as, for instance, souls, especially those of perfect animals. ②Now the second kind of wholeness is considered on the basis of the perfection of an essence, and is a wholeness to which essential parts correspond: the physical parts, matter and form, in the case of composites, and the logical parts, genus and difference; and this perfection is susceptible of degrees in the case of accidental forms, but not in the case of substantial forms. ③The third sort of wholeness is on a basis of power.[6] If, then, we were to speak of a given form which has extension in matter, such as "whiteness",

---

[6] Cf. *Q. De An.*, 10, resp.: "In a third sense the word 'whole' is used in reference to virtual or potential parts, and these parts are based on a division of activities."

[60]

Wholeness 1) based on quantity
2) based on perfection — essence
3) based on power

we might say that the whiteness is wholly in every part by a wholeness of essence and of power, but not by the first sort of wholeness, which belongs to it accidentally; thus the whole character of the species "whiteness" is found in every part of the surface; the total quantity which it accidentally possesses, however, is not, but part of this is in a part.

Now the soul,[7] and especially the human soul, does not have extension in matter. Hence the first sort of wholeness does not take place in it. The remaining alternative, therefore, is that from the viewpoint of wholeness of essence, it may be stated absolutely that it is wholly in every part of the body; not, however, from the viewpoint of wholeness of power, because the parts are perfected in different ways by the soul itself for different activities, and a definite activity belongs to it, namely, understanding, which it does not perform through any part of the body. And hence if the soul's wholeness is taken in the sense of wholeness of power, not only is the soul not wholly in every part, but neither is it wholly in the whole body; because the power of the soul exceeds the body's capacity, as has been said above [Art. II, Resp.].

As to the first argument, therefore, it must be said that the Philosopher in that passage is speaking of the soul with reference to its power of moving, which is primarily seated in the heart.

As to the second, it must be said that the soul is not in every part of the body primarily and essentially, but in relation to the whole, as has been said, and consequently not every part of an animal is an animal.

As to the third, it must be said that, according to the Philosopher in his book *De Somno et Vigilia* [I, 454a 8]: "An action belongs to that which has the potency for that action." And hence those powers whose activities do not belong to the soul alone but to the composite are in an organ as in a subject, but in the soul as in their root. Now, only those powers are in the soul as in a subject whose activities the soul does not carry out through an organ of the body; and yet these powers belong to the soul inasmuch as it is superior to the body. Hence it does not follow that all the powers of the soul are in every part of the body.

As to the fourth, it must be said that the form "house", since it is an accidental form, does not give specific actual being to the individual parts of the house, as the soul gives it to the individual parts of the body; and consequently there is no comparison.

---

[7] The general solution is valid also concerning the souls of more perfect brute animals; cf. *Contra Gentiles* II, cap. 72: "If, then, there is some form which is not divided by the division of its subject, and such are the souls of perfect animals, there will be no need of distinction, inasmuch as only one wholeness is applicable to them; but it must be said without qualification that this form is whole in every part of the body."

As to the fifth, it must be said that the passage there quoted is not understood to mean that the human soul is extended in correspondence with the body's extension, but that the virtual quantity of the soul does not reach out to a greater quantity than that of the body.

As to the sixth, it must be said that every activity is somehow understood as intermediate between the one who performs the activity and the object of the activity, either in reality (as in the case of those actions which go out from an agent to something external that is to be changed), or in a figurative sense, as, for instance, understanding, willing, and the like, which, although they are actions that remain within the agent, as is said in IX *Metaphysica* [8, 1050a 35], are nevertheless referred to after the fashion of other actions as tending from one thing to another. Thus, therefore, when someone is said to be acting in this or in that place, that statement can be understood in two senses. In one sense, that by adverbs of this sort the verb is modified from the standpoint of the activity going out from the agent, and in this sense it is true that wherever the soul acts, there it is. In another sense, from the standpoint of the activity's being understood as terminating in something else, and in this sense it is not true that wherever it acts there it is; for in this latter sense the soul feels and sees in the heavens, inasmuch as the heavens are felt and seen by it.

but isn't soul ← the mover of the body

As to the seventh, it must be said that the soul, when the body is moved, is moved accidentally and not of itself. Now it is not incongruous that a thing be at once moved and at rest accidentally, in different respects. It would, however, be incongruous if of itself it were at the same time at rest and being moved.

As to the eighth, it must be said that, although the soul is the act of every part of the body, nevertheless not all parts of the body are perfected by it in a uniform way, as has been said; but one part more notably and more perfectly than another.

As to the ninth, it must be said that a soul is said to be in a body through a definite shape, not in the sense that the shape is the cause of its being in the body, but rather the shape of the body results from the soul; and hence where there is no shape suited to "this soul", "this soul" cannot actually be. But the soul requires one shape in the whole body of which it is in a prior sense the act, and another in a part, of which it is the act in relation to the whole, as has been said. And hence in the case of animals in which the shape of a part is almost of the same form as the shape of the whole, a part receives the soul as a kind of whole; and therefore a part that has been cut off is alive. Yet in the case of perfect animals, in which the shape of a part would differ greatly from the shape of the whole, a part does not receive the soul as would something whole and primarily perfectible, so as to be alive when

[62]

cut off; it does nevertheless receive the soul in relation to the whole, so as to be alive when united to the whole.

As to the tenth, it must be said that an angel is related to the celestial body which it moves, not as a form but as a mover; and hence there is no comparison between it and the soul, which is the form of the whole and of every part.

As to the eleventh, it must be said that if the eye were in the foot, the power of sight would be there, because this power is the act of this kind of animate organ. But when the organ is removed, the soul remains there, but the power of sight does not.

As to the twelfth, it must be said that growth does not occur without local movement, as the Philosopher says in IV *Physica* [1, 209a 28; 6, 213b 4]. And hence when a boy grows, just as some part of the body begins to exist on its own account in a place where it previously was not, so also does the soul, in an accidental way, and by a changing over of itself, inasmuch as it is moved in an accidental way when the body is moved.

As to the thirteenth, it must be said that the organic body is perfectible by the soul primarily and essentially, whereas the individual organs and parts of organs are perfectible in relation to the whole, as has been said.

As to the fourteenth, it must be said that my flesh is more in agreement with your flesh, in view of its specific character, than is my flesh with my bone. But in comparison with the whole, the converse is true; for my flesh and my bone can be so ordered as to constitute one whole, whereas my flesh and your flesh cannot.

As to the fifteenth, it must be said that when a part is cut off, it does not follow that the soul is taken away, or that it is changed to another part, unless it were to be asserted that the soul was in that part alone; but it does follow that that part ceases to be perfected by the soul of the whole.

As to the sixteenth, it must be said that the soul is not indivisible as a point situated in a continuum is, to whose very character being in a divisible place would be contrary.[8] But the soul is indivisible by being quite apart from the whole genus "continuum"; and hence it is not contrary to its character if it be in some divisible whole.

As to the seventeenth, it must be said that in consequence of the very fact that it is indivisible, it follows that the soul does not have quantitative wholeness. Nor are we left on this account with the conclusion that there is in it merely a wholeness of powers; for there is in it a wholeness based on the character of its essence, as has been said.

----

[8] St. Thomas seems to have before him Avicenna's argument (*De An.* V, c. 2, *ab init.*).

As to the eighteenth, it must be said that the Philosopher in that book [*Met.* I] intends to investigate the principles of all beings, not only material principles, but also formal, efficient, and final ones. And consequently the natural philosophers of old, who laid down only a material cause, which has no place among incorporeal things, are refuted by him; and so they were not able to lay down the principles of all beings. He does not, therefore, intend to say that there is some material element of incorporeal things, but that those men are to be censured who neglected the principles of incorporeal things, laying down only a material cause.

As to the nineteenth, it must be said that in the case of those animals which live when cut in two, there is one soul in act and many in potency. Now through the act of cutting they are brought forth into actual many-ness, as happens in the case of all forms which have extension in matter.

As to the twentieth, it must be said that, when the soul is said to be wholly in every part, "whole" and "perfect" are understood on a basis of the character of the essence, and not on a basis of the character of power or excellence, as is clear from what has been said above.

ARTICLE V

THE fifth question is: Is there any created spiritual substance that is not united to a body?[1]

And it would seem not. *1* For Origen says in I *Peri Archon* [VI, PG XI, 170]: "It is proper to God alone, that is, to the Father, to the Son, and to the Holy Ghost that . . . He be understood to exist without any addition of a corporeal union." Therefore no created spiritual substance can exist that is not united to a body.

2 Furthermore, Pope Paschal says [*Decret.* II, 7, C. I, q. iii] that spiritual things cannot subsist apart from corporeal things. Therefore it is not possible for spiritual substances to exist that are not united to bodies.

3 Furthermore, Bernard in *Super Canticum* [*sermo* V, PL CLXXXIII, 800] says: "It is clear that every created spirit . . . needs bodily comfort." Now it is obvious that, since nature does not fall short in what is necessary, much less does God. Therefore no created spirit is found without a body.

4 Furthermore, if any created spiritual substance is entirely dissociated from a body, it must be above time, for time does not go beyond corporeal things. But created spiritual substances are not entirely above time. For since they have been created from nothingness and consequently take their beginning from change, they must be subject to change in such a way that they can lapse into non-being unless held together by some other being. Now that which can lapse into non-being is not wholly above time. For it can be at one time and not be at another. Therefore it is not possible for any created substances to be without bodies.

5 Furthmore, the angels assume certain bodies.[2] Now the body assumed by an angel is moved by it. Since, then, being moved locally presupposes sensation and life, as is clear from II *De Anima* [2-3], it would seem that the bodies assumed by angels have sensation and life,

---

[1] *Contra Gentiles* II, cap 46, 91,* 92; *De Potentia** VI, a. 6; *Summa Theol.* I, q. 50, a. 1; *In Lib. de Causis,* comm. 7; *De Subst. Separatis,* 18; *Compend. Theol.,* 74-75.

  Aristotle, XII, *Met.,* c. 8. St. Augustine (look in the index of the Maurine edition, under the heading "Angeli, an habeant corpora"). Avicebron, *Fons Vitae* III. Guil. Alvernus, *De Universo* II, 2, cc. 1-4. Alex. Halensis, *Summa* II, 1, pp. 131-133. Albertus M., II *Sent.,* d. 3, a. 1, vol. 27, p. 60. St. Bonaventure, *In II Sent.,* d. 1, p. 41; *Summa Philos.,* tr. 10, c. 1. The history of the controversy is adequately set forth in the *Dict. de théol. cath.,* art. "Anges." It is not usual for the definition of the Fourth Lateran Council (A.D. 1215, *Denz* 428) to be cited by the doctors of that time: "The creator of all things visible and invisible, spiritual and corporeal; Who by His own omnipotent power, right from the beginning of time created from nothing both creations, the spiritual and the corporeal; namely, the angelic and the mundane; and then the human, common to both, as it were, made up of spirit and body."

[2] Here St. Thomas is quoting rather freely from John Damascene (*De Fide Orth.* II, c. 27, PG XCIV, 959).

and so they are naturally united to bodies; and yet as regards the angels it would seem that they especially are free from bodies. Therefore there is no created spiritual substance which is not united to a body.

6 Furthermore, an angel is naturally more perfect than a soul. Now that which lives and gives life is more perfect than that which merely lives. Since, then, the soul lives and gives life to the body by the fact that it is its form, for all the greater reason it would seem that an angel not only lives but is also united to the same body to which it gives life; and thus we reach the same conclusion as before.

7 Furthermore, it is obvious that angels know singular things; otherwise it would be pointless to assign them to men as guardians. Now they cannot know singular things through universal forms, because in that event their knowledge would be the same with reference to the past and to the future, and this in spite of the fact that to know the future belongs to God alone. Accordingly angels know singular things through particular forms, which require corporeal organs wherein they may be received. Therefore angels have corporeal organs united to themselves; and thus it would seem that no created spirit is entirely free from a body.

8 Furthermore, the principle of individuation is matter. Now angels are individuals of a sort; otherwise they would not have actions of their own; for to act is characteristic of particular individuals. Since, then, they do not have matter of which they are constituted, as was said above, they seem to have matter wherein they exist, namely, the bodies to which they are united.

9 Furthermore, since created spirits are finite substances, they must be in a definite genus and species. Accordingly there is to be found in them the universal nature of a species. Now they do not receive their individuation from this universal nature itself. Therefore there must be something additional whereby they are individuated. Now this cannot be anything material which would enter into the composition of an angel, since angels are immaterial substances, as was said above. It must be the case, therefore, that some corporeal matter is added to them, whereby they are individuated; and thus we reach the same conclusion as before.

10 Furthermore, created spiritual substances are not merely matter, because in that case they would be in potency only and would not have any action; and in the second place they are not composed of matter and form, as was shown above [Art. I]. The only remaining alternative then is that they are merely forms. Now it is essential to a form that it be an act of matter to which it is united. It would seem, therefore, that created spiritual substances are united to corporeal matter.

[66]

11 Furthermore, when things are alike the same judgment is passed on them. But some created spiritual substances are united to bodies. Therefore all are.

But on the other hand there is *i* what Dionysius says in the fourth chapter [lec. 1] of *De Divinis Nominibus*, that angels are "incorporeal and immaterial."

ii Furthermore, according to the Philosopher in VIII *Physica* [5, 256b 20], if any two things are found connected, one of which can be found without the other, the second also must be found without the first. Now we do find a moved thing that is a mover, and hence, if something is moved but is not a mover, there is also to be found something that is a mover but not moved. But there is to be found something composed of bodily and of spiritual substance. Since, then, a body can be found that is without a spirit, it would seem that some spirit can be found that is not united to a body.

iii Furthermore, Richard of St. Victor [*De Trinitate* III, 9, *PL* CXCVI, 921] argues as follows: in the divine order several persons are found in one nature, whereas in the human order one person is found in two natures, namely, in soul and in body. Therefore[3] something intermediate is also to be found, namely, that one person is in one nature; and this would not be the case if a spiritual nature were united to a body.

iv Furthermore, an angel is in an assumed body. If, therefore, another body were naturally united to it, it would follow that two bodies would be in the same place at the same time, which is impossible. Therefore, there are some created spiritual substances which do not have bodies naturally united to themselves.

ANSWER. It must be said that, because our knowledge has its beginning from sensation and sensation belongs to corporeal things, from the beginning men searching out the truth were able to grasp only corporeal nature, to such an extent that the first natural philosophers used to think that nothing existed but bodies; and hence they also used to say that the soul itself is a body. The Manichaean heretics, who thought that God is a kind of corporeal light extended over infinite space, also seem to have followed them. So too the Anthropomorphites,[4] who fabricated God as a being formed with the features of the human body, surmised that nothing existed beyond bodies.

But later philosophers, transcending corporeal things in a rational way through the intellect, arrived at a knowledge of incorporeal sub-

---

[3] This conclusion "Therefore there is also to be found" is not drawn by Richard, at least not in the passage cited.
[4] Concerning the Anthropomorphites, see Augustine (*Epist.* 148, iv, *PL* XXXIII, 628), where he cites Jerome.

stance. First among these was Anaxagoras[5] who, because he asserted that from the beginning all corporeal things were mixed together, was forced to assert, in addition to the corporeal, something incorporeal and unmixed, which would differentiate and move corporeal things. And this he used to call "mind", which differentiates and moves all things, and we call it God. Plato, however, employed another way of asserting incorporeal substances. For he thought that prior to being which participates, something abstract and unparticipated should be asserted. And hence, since all bodies that can be sensed participate in those things which are predicated of themselves, namely, generic and specific natures and the natures of the other predicates universally applied to them, he asserted natures of this sort, abstracted from what is sensible and self-subsistent, and these he called "separated substances."

Arisotole, however [*Met.* XII, 8, 1073a], proceeded to assert separated substances as a result of the perpetuity of the movement of the heavens. For one must assign some end[6] for the movement of the heavens. Now, if the end of a given movement is not always constant in its mode of being, but it is moved of itself or accidentally, the movement must necessarily be lacking in uniformity. And hence the natural movement of heavy or of light bodies becomes stronger when it gets nearer to the state of "being in its proper place". Now we see that in the movements of heavenly bodies uniformity is always preserved, and from this he concluded to the perpetuity of the uniform movement. Accordingly he had to assert that the end of this particular movement was something that is not moved either of itself or accidentally. Now every body or anything else which is in a body is movable either of itself or accidentally. Thus, therefore, he had to posit some substance entirely separated from a body, which would be the end of the movement of the heavens.

Now the three positions mentioned above seem to differ in this respect: that Anaxagoras, on the basis of the principles laid down by him, did not consider it necessary to posit more than one incorporeal substance. Plato, however, considered it necessary to posit many substances that were mutually ordered according to the number and order of genera and species and of the other things which he posited as abstracts. For he posited a first abstract, which would be essentially the good and the one, and after that the different orders of intelligible things and of intellects. As for Aristotle, he posited several separated substances. For, since there appear in the heavens many movements of which he asserted

---

[5] These views of Anaxagoras are taken from various passages in Aristotle (*Met.* I, c. 3, 984ab; *Phys.* I, c. 4, 187a; *Phys.* VIII, c. 1, 250b, etc.). In the work *De Subst. Separatis* the various opinions are more fully set forth and compared with one another.

[6] Namely, that on account of which the movement takes place.

that every one was uniform and perpetual and for each and every movement there had to be a proper end, and since the end of a movement of this sort ought to be an incorporeal substance, the consequence was that he posited many[7] incorporeal substances, mutually ordered according to the nature and order of the movements of the heavens. Nor did he proceed further in asserting them, because it was characteristic of his philosophy not to depart from obvious data.

But those ways are not very suitable for us, because we do not assert with Anaxagoras the mixing of sensible things, nor with Plato the separateness of universals, nor with Aristotle the perpetuity of movement. Hence we must proceed by other ways to a demonstration of the point proposed.[8]

First then it is apparent that there are some substances wholly free from bodies, in consequence of the perfection of the universe. For the perfection of the universe seems to be such that it does not lack any nature which can possibly exist, and this is why [Genesis I] each thing is said to be good, and all things together exceedingly good.[9] Now it is obvious that if there are any two things, one of which does not depend on the other on the basis of its own character, it is possible for the one to be found apart from the other: thus, for instance, "animal" on the basis of its own character does not depend on "rational". And hence it is possible to find animals that are not rational. Now it is characteristic of substance to be self-subsistent, and it does not depend in any way on the character of "body", since the character of "body" is somehow related to certain accidents (namely, dimensions) by which subsistence is not caused. Therefore the only remaining alternative is that after God, Who is not included in any genus, there are to be found in the genus "substance" some substances which are free from bodies.

In the second place, the same consideration can be arrived at in consequence of the orderly arrangement of things, which is found to be such that we cannot go from one extreme to the other except through intermediates: thus, for instance, fire is found immediately beneath

---

[7] Following the astronomical theories of his time, Aristotle held the number "55" as more probable.

[8] Among the philosophers known to the mediaeval writers, the one who made the most elaborate attempt to demonstrate the existence of simple substances below God was Avicebron, whose treatise III (Fons Vitae) is nothing but "an assertion of simple substances;" namely, that (§1) "between the first high and holy maker and between the substance which supports the nine categories there is an intermediate substance"; and (§11) "there is not one substance but many." William of Auvergne (I, 1235) seems to have been the first theologian to develop arguments from reason that angels exist, and we know how highly he esteemed Avicebron. But in discussing this point St. Thomas does not mention Avicebron, but rather has reference to previous Scholastics, Pseudo-Dionysius, and the Liber de Causis.

[9] Cf. Augustine, Conf. XIII, xxviii, 43: "For individual things were merely good; but all things collectively were both good and exceedingly good."

"heavenly body", and beneath this air, and beneath this water, and beneath this earth, following the sequence of the nobility and subtility of these bodies. Now at the topmost summit of things there is a being which is in every way simple and one, namely, God. It is not possible, then, for corporeal substance to be located immediately below God, for it is altogether composite and divisible, but instead one must posit many intermediates, through which we must come down from the highest point of the divine simplicity to corporeal multiplicity. And among these intermediates, some are corporeal substances that are not united to bodies, while others, on the contrary, are incorporeal substances that are united to bodies.

Thirdly, the same is apparent from the special character of the intellect. For understanding is obviously an activity which cannot take place by means of the body, as is proven in III *De Anima* [4, 429ab]. And hence the substance whereof this is an activity must have actual being that does not depend on the body, but is raised above the body, for the activity of each thing corresponds to its being. If, therefore, some understanding substance is united to a body, it will not be so united insofar as it understands, but on some other basis; thus it was said above that it is necessary for the human soul to be united with a body insofar as it lacks the activities which are exercised through the body to make its intellectual activity complete, seeing that it understands by abstracting from phantasms. Actually this latter is something accidental to intellectual activity, and it pertains to its imperfection to get knowledge from things which are intelligible only in potency; just as it pertains to the imperfection of the sight of the bat that it has need to see in the dark. Now whatever is accidentally connected with a thing is not found with it in all cases. Besides, it must be the case that, prior to an imperfect being in a given genus, there is to be found a perfect being in that genus, because the perfect is naturally prior to the imperfect, as act is prior to potency. The only remaining alternative, then, is that one must posit some incorporeal substances that are not united to a body, as not needing a body for intellectual activity.[10]

As to the first argument, therefore, it must be said that on this point the quotation from Origen[11] is not acceptable; because he makes many

---

[10] Although the Angelic Doctor expounds these arguments so firmly and systematically, he certainly perceived that they prove no more than a kind of fitness, and in the *De Subst. Separatis,* leaving out all proofs from reason, he cites only authorities. This is an instance of the style of writing and type of speaking wherein he draws up and sets forth arguments that are merely probable along the lines of a demonstration. Cf. P. Rousselot, *L'intellectualisme de S. Thomas,* pp. 156 sqq. (2 edit., Paris, 1924).

[11] He says quite exactly in *De Pot.* VI, 6, ad 2: "And hence (Origen) seems to have been of the opinion that all incorporeal substances are united to bodies; although he does not assert this, but proposes it doubtfully, and also touches on another opinion."

erroneous statements in that book, following the views of the ancient philosophers.

As to the second, it must be said that Paschal is speaking of spiritual things with which temporal things are connected, and with the buying or selling of these latter, spiritual things themselves are understood to be bought or sold. For spiritual rights or consecrations do not have a subsistence of their own apart from the corporeal or temporal things that are connected with them.

As to the third, it must be said that every created spirit needs bodily comfort: some for their own sake, such as rational souls; others for our sake, such as the angels, who appear to us in assumed bodies.[12]

As to the fourth, it must be said that created spiritual substances, as regards their actual being, are said to be measured by eternity *(aevo)*, although their movements are measured by time, according to Augustine's statement in IV *Super Genesi ad Litteram* [VIII, 22, 43], "that God moves the spiritual creation during time." And as for the statement that created spiritual substance can be changed into non-being *(non esse)*, this has no reference to any potency existing in them, but to a power of the agent. For, just as before they existed they were able to exist only through the power of an agent, so, when they do exist, they can cease to exist only through the power of God, Who can take away His conserving hand. But in them there is no potency for non-being, such that they may be measured by time in the way in which things that can be moved, even though they are not moved, are measured by time.

As to the fifth, it must be said that to be moved locally by an intrinsic and conjoined moving power does presuppose sensation and life. But the bodies assumed by angels are not moved in this fashion; and hence the argument does not follow.

As to the sixth, it must be said that to live and give life as an efficient cause does is more noble than merely to live. But to give life as a formal cause does is characteristic of a substance less noble than one which lives with a subsistence of its own apart from a body. For the being of that intellectual substance which is the form of the body is rather something that is lowest and nearest to a corporeal nature, inasmuch as it can be communicated to it.

As to the seventh, it must be said that angels know particular things through universal forms, which are the likenesses of the ideal characters whereby God knows both universal things and singular things. Nevertheless they need not know the singulars which will exist, which have not yet participated in the nature and the form which is represented through the species of the angelic intellect. Now it is otherwise with

[12] Nevertheless in the sermon referred to St. Bernard openly contends that all angels have bodies conjoined to them.

the divine intellect, which, established in the eternal present, has a full view of all time in a single glance.

As to the eighth, it must be said that matter is the principle of individuation, inasmuch as it has not the natural capacity of being received in something else. But forms which have the natural capacity of being received in a subject cannot by themselves be individuated; because so far as their own character is concerned, it is a matter of indifference to them whether they are received in one or in many. But if there be a given form which is not able to be received in something, it has individuation from this very fact, because it cannot exist in many, but remains in itself by itself. And hence Aristotle in VII *Metaphysica* [14, 1039a 30] argues against Plato that if the forms of things are abstracts, they must be singular.

As to the ninth, it must be said that in things composed of matter and form the element of individuality adds to the specific nature a definite amount of matter and the individual accidents.[13] But in the case of separated forms the element of individuality does not really add anything to the specific nature, because in such forms the essence of the form is the self-subsistent individual itself, as the Philosopher makes clear in VII *Metaphysica* [*ibid.*]. Nevertheless it does add something conceptually, namely, the character of not being able to exist in many.

As to the tenth, it must be said that substances which are separated from bodies are merely forms; yet they are not acts of any matter. For, although matter cannot exist without form, yet form can exist without matter, because matter has existence through a form, and not vice versa.

As to the eleventh, it must be said that a soul, because it is the lowest among spiritual substances, has a greater affinity than higher substances with corporeal nature, so that it is able to be its form.

---

[13] In *Quodl.* II, a. 4 (Paris, 1269-1272) he teaches that the supposite adds something real, over and above the nature of the angels. In explaining this, John of Naples wrote (ca. 1323 A. D.): "He expressly says in his *Quodl.* II, 4 that in the angels the supposite differs from the nature, because in them the supposite also adds being over and above nature." Cf. *Xenia thom.* III, p. 89 (Rome, 1925).

ARTICLE VI

THE sixth question is: Is a spiritual substance united to a heavenly body?[1]

And it would seem that it is. *1* For Dionysius says in chapter seven [lect. 4] of *De Divinis Nominibus* that the divine wisdom "conjoins the ends of primary beings to the beginnings of secondary beings." And from this it can be gathered that a lower nature at its highest point touches a higher nature at its lowest point. Now the highest thing in corporeal nature is a heavenly body, and the lowest thing in spiritual nature is a soul. Therefore a heavenly body is animate.

2 Furthermore, the form of a more noble body is more noble. Now a heavenly body is the noblest of bodies, and a soul is the noblest of forms. If, therefore, some lower bodies are animate, much more will a heavenly body be animate.

But the objector said that, although a heavenly body is not animate, yet the form whereby that body is a body is more noble than the form whereby man's body is a body. But on the other hand, *3* either there is another substantial form in the human body beside the rational soul, which gives actual being to the body, or there is not. If there is not, but the soul itself gives actual substantial being to a body: since the soul is the noblest of forms, it will follow that the form through which the human body is a body is more noble than the form through which a heavenly body is a body. But if there should be another substantial form in man which gives actual being to the body besides a rational soul, it is obvious that through that form a human body is able to take on a rational soul. Now that which is able to take on perfect goodness is better than that which is not, as is said in II *De Caelo et Mundo* [12, 292b]. If, therefore, a heavenly body is not able to take on a rational soul, it will still follow that the form through which the human body is a body is more noble than the form through which the heavenly body is a body; which seems incongruous.

---

[1] *In II Sent.,* d. 14, q. 1, a. 3; *De Veritate* V, a. 9, ad 14; *Contra Gentiles* II c. 70;*Contra Gentiles* III,* c. 23, 24; *De Pot.** VI, a. 6; *Summa Theol.* I, q. 70, 3; *Q. De An.* 8, ad 3, ad 17, ad 18; *Quodl.* XII, a. 8; *In II De Caelo,* lec. 3 and 13; *In XII Met.,* lec. 9; *Resp. de 36 Articulos,* 1-3; *Resp. ad 42 Articulos,* 1-18.
    Aristotle, *De Caelo* II, c. 2; *Met.* XII, cc. 7-8. Avicenna, *Met.* IX, cc. 1-2. Algazel, I, tr. 4, cc. 2-3. Averroes, *In XII Met.,* comm. 44; *De Substantia Orbis,* c. 2; etc. Guil. Alvernus, *De Universo* II, 1, cc. 3-7, pp. 808 sqq. Albertus M., *Summa de Creat.* I, tr. 3, q. 16, a. 2, vol. 34, p. 439; *In II Sent.,* d. 14, a. 6, vol. 27, p. 265; *Summa Theol.* II, tr. 11, q. 53, m. 3, vol. 32, p. 566. St. Bonaventure, *In II Sent.,* d. 14, a. 3, q. 2, p. 347 (here, cf. the marginal note); *Summa Philos.,* tr. 15, cc. 10-13. Avicenna had said that heavenly bodies are informed by a sentient soul also, but Averroes that they were informed by an intellectual soul only. The more common belief among doctors at the time of St. Thomas was that they are not animated in the proper sense, yet are moved by angels. And this doctrine St. Thomas himself constantly professes, even if he does not always observe the same manner of speaking.

4 Furthermore, the perfection of the universe requires that to no body be denied that toward which it has a natural inclination. Now every body has a natural inclination toward that which it needs for its own activity. The proper activity, however, of a heavenly body is circular movement, and for this it stands in need of a spiritual substance: for this movement cannot be the consequence of any corporeal form, as are the movements of heavy and of light objects; because the movement would have to cease when it arrived at some definite place, as happens in the case of heavy and of light objects. This is clearly false. Therefore the only remaining alternative is that heavenly bodies have spiritual substances united to themselves.

5 Furthermore, every thing which, while existing in a particular condition, is naturally moved, cannot be at rest while existing in that same condition, save in a violent fashion; an example of this is a heavy or a light body that exists outside its own place. But if the movement of the heavens comes from a natural form, they must be naturally moved while existing in any place whatever; therefore, in whatever place it be said that they are at rest, they will not be at rest except through violence.[2] Now nothing violent can go on forever. Therefore the heavens are not forever at rest after the day of judgment as we assert according to faith. Since, therefore, this is incongruous, it would seem necessary to say that the heavens are moved by a voluntary movement. And so it follows that the heavens are animate.

6 Furthermore, in any genus that which exists of itself is prior to that which exists through something else. But the heavens are primary in the genus of movable things. Therefore they are moved of themselves, as self-moving movers. Now every self-moving mover is divided into two parts: one of which is that which does the moving through appetite, as, for example, the soul, and the other that which is the moved, as, for example, the body. Consequently a heavenly body is animate.[3]

7 Furthermore, nothing which is moved by an entirely extrinsic mover has a natural movement. Since, therefore, the movement of the heavens comes from a spiritual substance — because according to Augustine in III *De Trinitate* [IV, 9], God manages corporeal substance through spiritual substance — if that substance were not united to it, but were entirely extrinsic, the movement of the heavens would not be natural. This contradicts the Philosopher[4] in I *De Caelo* [8, 176b].

8 Furthermore, that spiritual substance which moves the heavens, if it were merely extrinsic, could not be said to move the heavens only

---

2 Cf. Aristotle, *De Caelo* II, c. 3, 286a.
3 Cf. the Philosopher, *Phys.* VIII, c. 4.
4 Cf. Aristotle, *De Caelo* II, c. 3, 286a, where the matter is put more clearly.

by willing; because in that case its willing would be its acting, which is characteristic of God alone. It accordingly would be necessary to impart something in order to produce motion; and in that case, since its power is limited, it would follow that fatigue would come upon it in its moving over a long course of time.[5] This is incongruous, and particularly so according to those who assert the eternity of movement. Therefore the spiritual substance which moves the heavens is united thereto.

9 Furthermore, as is held in IV *Physica* [VIII, 5], the movers of the lower spheres are moved accidentally, but the mover of the higher sphere is not. But the mover of a higher sphere is united to its own sphere as mover. Therefore the movers of the lower spheres are united to them not only as movers but as forms; and thus the lower spheres at least are animate.

10 Furthermore, as the Commentator says on XI *Metaphysica* [XII, comm. 48], the separated substances are in the best disposition in which they can possibly be: and this means that each one of them moves a heavenly body both as an agent and as an end. Now this could not be the case unless they were somehow united to them. Therefore incorporeal substances are united to the heavenly bodies; and thus the heavenly bodies would seem to be animate.

11 Furthermore, the Commentator, in the same book [comm. 25], expressly says that the heavenly bodies are animate.

12 Furthermore, nothing acts outside its own species; for an effect cannot be more powerful than its cause. Now living substance is better than non-living substance, as Augustine says in *De Vera Religione* [LV 109]. Since, therefore, heavenly bodies cause life, especially in the case of animals generated from putrefaction, it would seem that the heavenly bodies live and are animate.

13 Furthermore, the Commentator says in his book *De Substantia Orbis* [II] that "circular movement is proper to the soul." Therefore those bodies especially seem to be animate for which it is natural to be moved in a circular fashion. Now such are the heavenly bodies. Therefore the heavenly bodies are animate.

14 Furthermore, to praise, to show forth *(enarrare)*, and to rejoice are proper only to an animate and knowing thing. But the aforesaid actions are attributed to the heavens in Holy Scripture, according to the *Psalm* [CXLVIII, 4]: "Praise him, ye heavens of heavens;" [XVIII, 1]: "The heavens show forth the glory of God;" and *Apocalypse* XIV [XVIII, 20]: "Rejoice over her, thou heaven." Therefore the heavens are animate.[6]

---

[5] Cf. Aristotle, II, c. 1, 284a 17.
[6] This is the argument of Rabbi Moses; cf. Q. *De An.* 8, ad 19.

But on the other hand there is *i* what Damascene says in book II [*De Fide Orth.*, VI, *PG* XCIV, 886] : "Let no one think that the heavens or the stars are animate; for they are inanimate and insensible."

ii Furthermore, a soul united to a body is not separated from it save by death. But the heavenly bodies cannot be mortal, since they are incorruptible. Therefore if some spiritual substance be united to them as souls, they will be perpetually bound to them; and this seems incongruous, that some angels should be perpetually assigned to some bodies.

iii Furthermore, the heavenly society of the blessed consists of angels and of souls. But the souls of the heavens, if the heavens are animate, are included in neither division. Therefore there would be some rational creatures which cannot be participants in beatitude; and this seems incongruous.

iv Furthermore, every rational creature, considered according to its own nature, is able to sin. If, then, some rational creatures are united to heavenly bodies, there would be nothing against some one of them having sinned, and thus it would follow that some one of the heavenly bodies is moved by an evil spirit; which seems absurd.

v Furthermore, we ought to implore the intercession of the good spirits. If, then, some spirits are united to heavenly bodies, since it is not fitting to assert that they are evil, but it should be asserted that they are good, seeing that they assist God in the management of corporeal nature, it would follow that their intercession ought to be implored. But it would seem absurd if anyone were to say "O Sun" or "O Moon, pray for me." It should, therefore, not be asserted that some spirits are united to heavenly bodies.

vi Furthermore, a soul holds together the body to which it is united, according to the Philosopher in I *De Anima* [5, 411b 7]. If, then, heavenly bodies are animate, it would follow that some created spiritual substance holds together the whole heavens: and this is absurd, since this is characteristic of Uncreated Wisdom alone, in Whose person it is said in *Ecclesiasticus* XXIV [8] : "I alone have compassed the circuit of the heavens."

ANSWER. It must be said that concerning this question there have been different opinions, both among the ancient philosophers and also among the doctors of the Church. Anaxagoras, however, thought that the heavenly bodies were inanimate; and hence he was killed by the Athenians, for he said, "The sun is a stone on fire."[7] But Plato and Aristotle and their followers asserted that the heavenly bodies are animate. Likewise also among the doctors of the Church, Origen asserted that the heavenly

---

[7] Cf. Diog. Laert. II, 8, but St. Thomas had this from Augustine (*De Civitate Dei* XVIII, 41) and he refers to this passage in *Summa Theol.* I, q. 70, a. 3.

bodies are animate. And Jerome followed him, as is clear from a certain gloss on *Ecclesiastes* I [6] : "The spirit goeth forward surveying all in its circuit."[8] However, Damascene affirms that heavenly bodies are inanimate, as is clear from the passage quoted above. But Augustine leaves the question doubtful in II *Super Genesi ad Litteram* [XVIII, 38] and in his *Enchiridion* [LVIII].

Both opinions, however, have the character of probability. For the consideration of the nobility of the heavenly bodies leads to asserting that they are animate, since in the genus of "things" living things are preferred to all non-living things. But the consideration of the nobility of spiritual substances leads us to the contrary view. For higher spiritual substances cannot have any of the activities of the soul except those which pertain to the intellect: because the other activities of life are the acts of the soul insofar as it is the form of a corruptible and changeable body; for these activities take place along with a certain change and corporeal alteration. Nor does the intellect of higher substances seem to need to get knowledge from sensible things, as our intellect does. If, therefore, none of the activities of life are in them except understanding and willing, which do not need a corporeal organ, their dignity would seem to exceed union with a body. Of these two considerations, however, the second is more effective than the first. For the union of soul and body does not take place for the sake of the body, namely, that the body may be ennobled, but for the sake of the soul, which needs the body for its own perfection, as was said above [Art. II, Obj. 5].

Now, if one studies the matter more closely, he will perhaps find that there is either little or no discrepancy between these two opinions; and this is to be understood as follows. For it cannot be said that the movement of a heavenly body is a consequence of some corporeal form, as movement upwards is a consequence of the form "fire". For it is obvious that a single natural form tends toward but one thing. Now the character of movement is at variance with oneness, because it is of the essence of movement that a thing should be otherwise in the present and at a previous time. And hence a natural form does not tend toward movement for the sake of the movement itself but for the sake of being in some place, and when this has been reached the movement ceases; and this is what would happen in the case of the movement of the heavens if it were a consequence of some natural form. One should say then that the movement of the heavens comes from some intelligent substance. For the end of this movement can only be a certain abstract intelligible good,

---

8 Cf *PL* XXIII, 1016: "or if he has called the sun itself 'spirit' because it gives life (some codices read: Because it is animal), and breathes, and has strength." The passage is cited by St. Thomas, *De Veritate* V, 9, ad 14: "He has called the sun 'spirit' because, like an animal, it breathes and has strength." Elsewhere Jerome does not teach that the heavens are animate.

for the sake of which the intelligent substance which moves the heavens does its moving, namely, in order that it may take on a likeness of that good in its working and in order that what is virtually contained in that intelligible good may be made explicit in act; and especially the filling up of the number of the Elect, for whose sake all other things seem to exist.[9]

Thus, then, there will be two orders of spiritual substances. Some of these will be movers of the heavenly bodies and are united to them as movers are to movable things, as Augustine also says in III *De Trinitate* [IV, 9] that all bodies are ruled by God through the rational spirit of life; and the same view is held by Gregory in IV *Dialogi* [VI, *PL* LXXVII, 329]. But some substances will be ends of these movements, and these are wholly abstracted and not united to bodies; but others are united to heavenly bodies in the way in which a mover is united to a mobile thing. This seems to suffice for preserving the meaning of Plato and of Aristotle. With respect to Plato, this point is obvious; for Plato, as has been said above, did not say that even the human body is animate in any other sense except insofar as the soul is united to the body as a mover. But from the statements of Aristotle it is obvious that he did not assert in the heavenly bodies any of the virtues of the soul save the intellectual. But the intellect according to him is not the act of any body.

Now to say further that heavenly bodies are animate in this way, like lower bodies which grow and sense through a soul, is contrary to the incorruptibility of the heavenly bodies. Thus, then, it must be denied that heavenly bodies are animate in the way in which lower bodies are animate. But it must not be denied that the heavenly bodies are animate, if by animation nothing else is meant than the union of a mover to a mobile thing.[10] Augustine seems to touch on these two ways in II *Super Genesi ad Litteram* [XVIII]; for he says: "It is usually asked whether

---

[9] The moving angel, understanding and desiring some higher good (whether God or a higher angel), aims at assimilating himself to that good in his activity, by producing the most perfect movement of his own sphere, that is, the circular, by which movement the process of generation and corruption is carried forward in this sublunar world, particularly the generation and evolution of men, in order that the number of the Elect may be completed. In the following passages St. Thomas favors the view (of Averroes in *Met.* XII; cf. below, ad 10) which assigns to the individual spheres, besides an angel who moves as an efficient cause, another higher angel which is aimed at by that one as its end. So also in *II Sent.*, d. 14, q. 1, a. 3: "On this point, moreover, (the position of the philosophers) can be upheld, so that we may say that higher angels, which have more universal forms, are separate and remote movers; whereas lower angels, which have more particular forms, . . . are proximate movers." Yet for the most part he says nothing about remote movers.

[10] In *Respons. ad 42 Articulos* (ad 3) he says: "I remember having read that the statement: heavenly bodies are moved by a spiritual creature, was denied by no one of the saints or philosophers." Yet the difficulties raised in that passage and in *Respons. ad lect. Venetum* (made up of 36 articles) show that some of his contemporaries doubted this.

[78]

the stars of the heavens are those conspicuous bodies alone, or whether they have certain ruling spirits of their own; and if they have, whether they are also vitally inspired by them, as bodies are animated by the souls of animals." But although he himself leaves both suppositions doubtful, as is clear from what follows, it must be said according to the above considerations that they have ruling spirits, by which nevertheless they are not animated in the same fashion as lower animals are animated by their souls.

As to the first argument, therefore, it must be said that a heavenly body borders on spiritual substances, insofar as a lower order of spiritual substances is united to the heavenly bodies after the manner of a mover.

As to the second, it must be said that according to Averroes' view the heavens are composed of matter and form, just as an animal is among lower beings. But "matter" is nevertheless used equivocally in both instances: for in higher things it is not a potency toward actual being as in lower things, but only toward place. Hence an actually existing body is itself matter, and does not need a form to give it actual being, since it is actually a being *(ens actu)*, but only to give it motion. And so a heavenly body has a more noble form than a human body, but in another way. If, however, it be said, as others say, that a heavenly body is itself composed of matter and corporeal form, then one will still be able to say that that corporeal form will be the most noble, inasmuch as it is a form and an act which fulfils the whole potentiality of matter, so that there does not remain in it a potentiality to another form.

And through this the solution to the third is also clear.

As to the fourth, it must be said that from the fact that a heavenly body is moved by a spiritual substance, it follows that it has an inclination toward the substance itself as toward a mover, and not otherwise.

And the same thing must be said as to the fifth and the sixth.

As to the seventh, it must be said that a spiritual substance which moves the heavens has a natural power which is determined with respect to the movement of such a body; and likewise the body of the heavens has a natural aptitude for being moved by such a movement. And on this account the movement of the heavens is natural, although it comes from an intelligent substance.

As to the eighth, it must be said that there is probability in the statement that a spiritual substance moves a heavenly body by a command of the will. For although in regard to a change of form corporeal matter does not obey a created spirit according to the will of the latter, but obeys only God, as Augustine says in III *De Trinitate* [viii, 13], yet the fact that it can obey such a spirit according to its will in regard to a change of place is evident even in the case of ourselves, in whom, immediately after a command of the will, there follows a movement of our bodily members. If nevertheless over and above a command of the will there should be added also the influence of some power, there is not on this account any fatigue that follows from the limited character of the power; for every power of a higher order, although it is limited in itself and in relation to something higher than itself, is nevertheless unlimited in relation to its own inferiors,[11] as, for instance, the power of the sun also is unlimited in relation to things capable of generation and corruption, and through the production of these things, even if it were to go on forever, it would not be lessened; and similarly the virtue of the intellect is unlimited in relation to sensible forms. And so too the power of a spiritual substance which moves the heavens is unlimited in relation to corporeal movement; and hence fatigue in it does not follow.

As to the ninth, it must be said that the soul which moves corruptible animals is united to them in respect of their actual being, but the spiritual substance which moves the heavenly bodies is united to them merely in respect of their being moved. And hence being moved accidentally is attributed to the soul of a corruptible animal by reason of its very self. For when the body with which it is one in being is moved, it must itself be moved accidentally. But being moved accidentally is attributed to the mover of a lower sphere, not by reason of its very self, but by reason of the mobile thing, insofar, that is, as the lower sphere is moved accidentally, as having been brought downward by the movement of the higher sphere. But the mover of a higher sphere is not moved accidentally in either way, because its sphere is not brought downward but brings others downward.

As to the tenth, it must be said on this point we find that Averroes has expressed different views. For in the book *De Substantia Orbis* [1, *post med.*], he said that what moves the heavenly bodies as agent and as end is one and the same; and this is surely quite erroneous, particularly in relation to the view whereby he asserts that the first cause is not above the substances that move the first heaven.[12] For on this view it follows that God is the soul of the first heaven, inasmuch as the substance which moves the first heaven as agent is called its soul. And the argument on which he made this statement is very inadequate: for because in the case of substances separated from matter the thing that understands and the thing that is understood are the same, he thought that the thing which desires and the thing which is desired are the same; and there is no parallel here. For knowledge of anything whatever takes place according as the thing known is in the knower; but desire takes place by way of a turning of the desirer toward the thing

---

[11] Cf. *Liber de Causis*, §15.
[12] For he says that God Himself is the mover of the first sphere, while Avicenna affirms that the first heaven is moved by the first created intelligence.

desired. Now if the good desired were present in the desirer of its very self, it would not be proper to it to do any moving toward the attainment of the desired good. And hence one should say that the desired good, which moves as an end, is something other than the desirer, which moves as an agent. And this, too, is the very same statement which the Commentator makes on XI *Metaphysica* [XII, comm. 38; 41]; for there he asserts two movers: one conjoined, which he calls the soul, and the other separated, which moves as an end. Nevertheless from all this we get nothing more than the fact that a spiritual substance is united to a heavenly body as its mover.

As to the eleventh, it must be said that he says heavenly bodies are animate, because spiritual substances are united to them as movers, and not as forms.[13] Hence on VII *Metaphysica* [comm. 31], he says that the formative power of semen "does not act save through the heat which is in the semen, not in the sense of being a form in it, like the soul in natural heat, but in the sense of being enclosed there, as a soul is enclosed in heavenly bodies."

As to the twelfth, it must be said that a heavenly body, inasmuch as it is moved by a spiritual substance, is its instrument. And so it does its moving in virtue of a spiritual substance to produce life in those lower bodies, just as a saw acts in virtue of an art to make a box.

As to the thirteenth, it must be said that from this reasoning nothing more can be gathered than that the heavenly bodies are moved by spiritual substances.

As to the fourteenth, it must be said that according to Damascene the heavens are said to show forth the glory of God, to praise, or to rejoice, in a material sense, insofar as they are, for men, the matter of praising or showing forth or rejoicing. For similar sayings are found in the Scriptures about mountains, hills, and other inanimate creatures.

But as to the first of the objections which are raised to the contrary, it must be said that Damascene denies that the heavenly bodies are animate in the sense that spiritual substances are united to them as forms, as to corruptible living things.

As to *ii*, it must be said that one angel is assigned to the guardianship of one man for as long as he lives; and hence there is no incongruity if one angel is assigned to move a heavenly body for as long as it is moved.

---

[13] *In II Sent.*, d. 14, i, 3, and in *De Ver.* V, ad 14, he does not want them to be called forms. In *De Pot.* VI, a. 6, the matter is not entirely clear. Moreover, he writes in *Contra Gentiles* II, c. 72: "It will be necessary to say that the intellect is substantially united to a heavenly body as a form"; and similarly in *Q. De An.* 8, ad 3. But, as here, so in *Summa Theol.* I, q. 70, a. 3, he again finds fault with the word "form": "But in order that it may do its moving, it need not be united to it as a form, but through the contact of power, as a mover is united to a mobile thing."

As to *iii*, it must be said that, if heavenly bodies are animate, the spirits presiding over them are counted among the company of the angels. Hence Augustine says in his *Enchiridion* [LVIII, *PL* XL, 260]: "Nor do I know for certain whether the sun, the moon, and all the stars belong to the company of the angels; although to some they may seem to be luminous bodies, not having sense or intelligence."

As to *iv*, it must be said that on this point there is no doubt, if we follow the opinion of Damascene [*De Fide Orth*. II, 4, *PG* XCIV, 875], who asserts that the angels who sinned belonged to the number of those who are set over corruptible bodies. But if, according to Gregory's belief, some of the higher also sinned, it must be said that God preserved from a fall those whom he appointed to this service, as He did many of the others also.

As to *v*, it must be said that we do not say: "O Sun, pray for me," both because a spiritual substance is not united to the body of the heavens as a form but merely as a mover, and also to remove all occasion of idolatry.

As to *vi*, it must be said that according to the Philosopher in IV *Physica* [VIII, 10, 267b 7], the mover of the heavens is in some part of them, and not in the whole; and so it does not compass the circuit of heaven. But it is otherwise with the soul, which gives being to the body as a whole and in its parts.

ARTICLE VII

THE seventh question is: Is a spiritual substance united to an ethereal body?[1]

And it would seem. that it is. 1 For Augustine says in III *Super Genesi ad Litteram* [X, 14] and in IV *De Civitate Dei* [VIII, 16; XV, 23] that demons have ethereal bodies. But demons are spiritual substances. Therefore a spiritual substance is united to an ethereal body.

2 Furthermore, Augustine says in his book *De Divinatione Daemonum* [III, 7, *PL* XL, 584] that demons are beyond the human senses because of the subtility of an ethereal body. Now this would not be the case, unless they were naturally united to an ethereal body. Therefore spiritual substances are united to an ethereal body.

3 Furthermore, the mean does not differ widely from the extremes. But in the region of heavenly bodies life is found, according to those who assert that the heavenly bodies are animate; and in the region of earth life is found in animals and in plants. Therefore in the middle region also, that of the air, life is found. Nor can this have reference to bird life, because birds are raised above the earth a little distance in the air, and it would not seem fitting that all the other air space should remain devoid of life. One must then assert, as it seems, that some ethereal living beings exist in it, from which it follows that some spiritual substances are united to an ethereal body.

4 Furthermore, a body that is more noble has a more noble form. But air is a more noble body than earth, inasmuch as it is more formal and more fine. If then a spiritual substance such as the soul is united to an earthly body, namely, a human body, for all the greater reason would it be united to an ethereal body.

5 Furthermore, in the case of things which agree more closely, union is easier. But "air" seems to agree more with "soul" than does a mixed body, such as man's body is; because, as Augustine says in *Super Genesi ad Litteram* [VII, 15 and 19], the soul manages the body through air. Therefore the soul is naturally more apt to be united to an ethereal body than even to a mixed body.

6 Furthermore, it is said in the book *De Substantia Orbis* [of Averroes, II]: "Circular movement is characteristic of the soul," and this for the reason that the soul, so far as it is itself concerned, is disposed to do its moving in all directions without any difference. But this also

---

[1] *In II Sent.*, d. 8, q. 1, a. 1; *Contra Gentiles* II, cap. 90, 91; *De Pot.* VI, 6; *Summa Theol.* I, q. 51, a. 1; *De Malo,** XVI, 1; *De Subst. Separatis,* 18-19.
  St. Augustine (in various passages where he is recording the views of the Platonists, which he sometimes seems to approve of, at least as regards demons). Guil. Alvernus, *De Universo* II, 2, cc. 5, 27, 28. Alex. Halensis, *Summa* II, 1, p. 238. St. Bonaventure, *In II Sent.*, d. 8, p. 210. Albertus M., *In II Sent.*, d. 8, A, a. 1, vol. 27, p. 168. *Summa Philos.* tr. 10, c. 1 and following.

seems to be characteristic of the air, because it is light in combination with light objects and heavy in combination with heavy objects. Therefore the soul would seem most of all to be united to air.

But on the other hand, the soul is the act of an organic body. But an ethereal body cannot be organic because, since it cannot be bounded by a boundary of its own but only by the boundary of something else, it cannot have any shape. Therefore a spiritual substance, which the soul is, cannot be united to an ethereal body.

ANSWER. It must be said that it is impossible for a spiritual substance to be united to an ethereal body.[2] This can be clearly shown in three ways. In the first place, because among all other bodies the simple bodies of elements are the more imperfect,[3] since they are like matter in relation to all other bodies. And hence it is not consistent with the scheme of things for some simple elementary body to be united to a spiritual substance as a form. The second reason is that air is a body, which is homogeneous as a whole and in all its parts. Hence if some spiritual substance is united to any one part of the air, for the same reason it will also be united to the whole air, and likewise to every other element, which seems absurd. The third reason is that a spiritual substance is found to be united to a given body in two ways: in one way, in order to furnish movement to a body, as, for instance, it was said that spiritual substances are united to the heavenly bodies; in another way, in order that a spiritual substance may be helped by a body as regards its own proper activity, which is understanding, as a human soul, for instance, is united to a body in order that it may acquire a store of knowledge through the bodily senses. But a spiritual substance cannot be united to the air; not by reason of movement, because air has a certain connatural movement which is a consequence of its natural form, nor is there to be found any movement in the whole air or in any part thereof which cannot be referred back to some bodily cause; and hence from its movement it does not appear that a spiritual substance is united to it. Nor yet is a spiritual substance united to an ethereal body for the perfection of intellectual activity: for a simple body cannot be an instrument of sense, as is proven in *De Anima* [III, 12, 434b 10]. Hence the only remaining alternative is that spiritual substance is in no way united to a body.

---

[2] But we must note that it is an entirely different question whether angels can ever assume ethereal bodies, of which they are the movers and not the forms; and this is admitted. Cf. *Summa Theol.* I, q. 51, a. 2-3.

[3] In *De Malo* (XVI, 1, resp.) St. Thomas warns us that "the Peripatetics, Aristotle's followers, did not assert that there are demons." And there he admits (ad 3) that "It is probable enough that Dionysius, who was in many respects a follower of the Platonist view, thought in company with them that demons are a kind of living beings which have sense-appetite and sense-knowledge", and in ad 7 he thinks that Damascene held with Origen that demons have bodies.

As to the first argument, therefore, it must be said that wherever Augustine says that demons have ethereal bodies, he does not say so as an assertion of his own belief, but according to the opinion of others. And hence he himself says in XII *De Civitate Dei* [X, 1]: "Even demons have a kind of body of their own, as learned men have thought, of that thick and humid air . . . But if anyone should assert that demons have no bodies, there is no need either to work out a laborious investigation of this matter or to quarrel about it in contentious argument."

And through this the solution to the second is clear.

As to the third, it must be said that the place for the mixing of the elements is in the lower region, namely, that around the earth. Now mixed bodies, the closer they come to an equal mixture, the farther do they recede from the extremes of contraries; and thus they acquire a kind of likeness to the heavenly bodies, which are without contrariety. And so it is clear that life is more able to exist in the highest and in the lowest region than in the middle one; especially when, in the case of those lower ones, the body is all the more prepared for life the nearer it comes to an equality of constituency.

As to the fourth, it must be said that the body "air" is more noble than the body "earth." But a body of equal constituency is more noble than both, because it is more distant from contrariety; and this kind of body only is found to be united to a spiritual substance. In it, nevertheless, the lower element must be materially more abundant in order to constitute equality, on account of the excess of active power in the other elements.

As to the fifth, it must be said that a soul is said to manage its own body through air so far as movement is concerned, because air is more susceptible to movement than are other dense bodies.

As to the sixth, it must be said that air is not indifferent to every movement, but in combination with certain bodies it is light, in combination with others it is heavy; and hence from this we cannot conclude that air is perfectible through a soul.

ARTICLE VIII

THE eighth question is: Do all angels differ in species from one another?[1]

And it would seem that they do not. *1* Augustine says in his *Enchiridion* [XXIX]: "The rational creaturehood which was in men, since by reason of sins and penalties . . . it had wholly perished" deserved "in part to be renewed." And from this it is argued as follows. If all angels were different from one another in their specific nature, then, since many angels fell irreparably, many natures would have irreparably perished. But Divine Providence does not allow any rational nature to perish entirely, as is clear from the passage quoted. Therefore not all angels differ from one another in specific nature.

2 Furthermore, the closer some things are to God, in Whom there is no diversity, the less different they are. Now according to the order of nature angels are closer to God than men are. But beings which differ numerically and specifically are more different from one another than are those which differ numerically and agree specifically. Since, therefore, men do not differ specifically, but only numerically, it would seem that angels too do not differ specifically.

3 Furthermore, an agreement of things in their formal principle causes them to be specifically the same, but a difference in their material principle makes them differ only numerically. Now in angels their very existence serves as the formal element with regard to the angel's essence, as has been said above. Since then all angels agree in existence but differ in essence, it would seem that angels differ, not specifically, but only numerically.

4 Furthermore, every subsisting created substance is an individual, included under some nature common to a species in such a way that if the individual be a composite, the specific nature will be predicated of it according to its character as a composite, but if the individual is simple, the specific nature will be predicated of it in consideration of its simple characteristics. Now an angel is a subsisting created substance. Whether, then, it be composed of matter and form or whether it be simple, it must be included under some specific nature. But the fact that it can have many supposites does not detract from a specific nature;

---

[1] *De Ente et Essent.*, 5; *De Natura Materiae*, 3; *In II Sent.**, d. 3, q. 1, a. 4-5; *In IV Sent.*, d. 12, q. 1, a. 1, sol. 3, ad 3; *Contra Gentiles* II, cap. 93, 95; *Summa Theol.** I, q. 50, a. 4; *Q. De An.* 7 (indirectly); *In Librum de Causis*, lec. 4; *De Unit. Intell.* 5, §105 (but very roughly); *De Subst. Separatis* 8; *Quodl.* II, a. 4.
    Avicenna, *Met.* V, c. 2; IX, c. 4. Algazel, tr. IV, c. 3, *ad fin. Liber de Causis*, §4. Guil. Alvernus, *De Universo* II, 2, cc. 9-12, p. 852. Alex. Halensis, *Summa* II, 1, p. 154. Albertus M., *Summa de Creat.* I, tr. 4, q. 28, a. 2, vol. 34, pp. 495-496; *In II Sent.*, d. 3, A, a. 5, vol. 27, p. 69; *ibid.*, d. 9, a. 7, p. 203. St. Bonaventure, *In II Sent.*, d. 3, p. 1, a. 2, q. 1, p. 102; *ibid.*, d. 9, a. 1, q. 1. (Among the articles censured at Paris in the year 1277 was this (42): "That God could not multiply individuals within one species without matter.")

so too the fact of having something like itself in the same species does not detract from an individual existing under such a nature. Therefore it would seem to be possible that there are many angels belonging to one species. But in the case of eternal beings there is no difference between "actual" and "possible", as is said in III *Physica* [4, 203b 30]. Therefore, among the angels there are many individuals of a single species.

5 Furthermore, among the angels there is perfect love *(dilectio)*; accordingly nothing which pertains to the perfection of love must be taken away from them. But the fact that there are many belonging to one species pertains to the perfection of love, because all living beings of one species naturally love one another, according to the words of *Ecclesiasticus* XIV [XIII, 19] "Every living being loveth its like." Therefore in the case of angels there are many belonging to one species.

6 Furthermore, since a species alone has a definition, according to Boethius [*In Porphyr., PL* LXIV, 79D], all things which agree in their definition would seem to agree in their species. But all angels agree in that definition which Damascene lays down in his third book [II *De Fide Orth.*, 3, *PG* XCIV, 866]: "An angel is an intellectual substance, always mobile, free in its will, incorporeal, serving God, receiving immortality in consequence of grace (not by nature)."[2] Therefore all angels belong to one species.

7 Furthermore, according to the order of nature angels are closer to God than men are. But in God there are three persons of numerically one nature. Since then there are, among men, many persons of one specific nature, it would seem that for all the greater reason among the angels there are many persons agreeing in one specific nature.

8 Furthermore, Gregory says [*Homil. in Evang.* XXXIV, *PL* LXXVI, 1255C] that in that heavenly country where there is a fullness of good, although certain attributes have been bestowed in an outstanding degree, yet none of these is possessed in an individual way; for all attributes are in all, not indeed equally, since some angels possess them in a more sublime degree than others, and yet all have them. There is, therefore, no difference in angels except one of "more and less". But "more and less" do not constitute a specific difference. Therefore angels do not differ specifically.

9 Furthermore, things which agree in what is most noble agree in species, because that which puts something in a species is more noble than that which puts a thing in a genus; for a specific difference is something formal in relation to a genus. But all angels agree in the most noble thing that is in them, namely, in intellectual nature. Therefore all angels agree in species.

---

[2] The reading in Migne is ἐν τῇ φύσει not οὐ τῇ φύσει.

10   Furthermore, if a given genus is divided by two differences, one of which is more imperfect than the other, the more imperfect difference is more capable of multiplication than is the more perfect; thus, for instance, "irrational" is multiplied in more species than is "rational". Now spiritual substance is divided by "capable of union" (*unibile*) and "not capable of union" *(non unibile)*; but "capable of union with a body" is something more imperfect, in the case of spiritual substances. Since then a spiritual substance capable of union with a body, namely, the human soul, is not divided into many species, for all the greater reason a spiritual substance which is not capable of union, namely, an angel, is not multiplied in many species.

11   Furthermore, Pope Boniface [*Epist.* II, *PL* LXV, 43-44] says that ministerial functions in the church militant are modelled after the heavenly host, wherein angels differ in orders and in power. But in the church militant, a difference in orders and in power does not make men differ specifically. Therefore, neither in the heavenly host of angels do angels differ specifically, even those who are of different orders or hierarchies.

12   Furthermore, just as the lower elements are adorned with plants and animals, and the sidereal heaven with stars, sun, and moon, so too the empyrean heaven is adorned with angels. But among plants and animals many of the same species are found; likewise also it would seem that all the stars belong to the same species, because they share in one most noble form, which is light. Therefore it would seem by a parallel argument that either all angels or some angels agree in one species.

13   Furthermore, if many angels are not asserted to agree in one species, this is only because there is no matter in them. But the removal of matter not only takes away plurality of individuals, but also their unity: because an individual is not put into a species except through matter, because matter is the principle of individuation. If, therefore, it must be asserted that angels are individuals in some sense, by a parallel argument it can also be asserted that there are many in one species.

14   Furthermore, "in those things which are separated from matter, the being which understands and that which is understood are the same," according to the Philosopher [III *De An.,* 4, 430a 3]. If, then, angels were without matter, the angel which understands and the angel which is understood would be the same. But every angel understands every other angel. Therefore it would follow that there is but one angel, which is false. One must not, therefore, assert that angels are without matter, and so neither must it be asserted that all the angels differ specifically.

15 Furthermore, number is a species of quantity, which is not apart from matter. If, then, there were no matter in the angels, there would be no number in them, which is false. Therefore we reach the same conclusion as before.

16 Furthermore, in those things which are without matter there is no multiplication except on a basis of cause and effect, as Rabbi Moses says [*Dux perplex.* I, 79].[3] If, then, angels are without matter, either there is no manyness among them or one is the cause of another; and both these alternatives are false. Therefore we reach the same conclusion as before.

17 Furthermore, creatures have been created by God in order that the divine goodness may be represented in them. But in a single species of "angel" the divine goodness is more perfectly represented than in the single species of "man". Therefore, one should not posit many species of angels.

18 Furthermore, different species which are divided as a result of being opposites differ by a specific difference. Now it is impossible to indicate a number of opposite specific differences as great as the multitude of the angels is asserted to be. Therefore not all angels differ specifically.

But on the other hand, *i* if some angels agree specifically, this would seem to be particularly the case with those who are of one order. But those who are of one order do not agree specifically, since there are in the same order "the first, the intermediate, and the last," as Dionysius says in the tenth chapter of *De Caelesti Hierarchia* [§1; rather IV, *PG* I, 194A]. A species, however, is not predicated of its own individuals in an order of sequence, as is said in III *Metaphysica* [3, 999a 6]. There are not, therefore, many angels of one species.

ii Furthermore, only those things which are corruptible would seem to be multiplied numerically in one species, in order that the specific nature, which cannot be preserved in one, may be preserved in many. But the angels are incorruptible. Therefore there are not many angels of one species.

iii Furthermore, the multiplication of individuals in one species takes place through a division of matter. But the angels are immaterial, because, as Augustine says in XIII *Confessiones* [XII, 7], matter is "next to nothing", whereas the angels are "next to God." Therefore in angels there is no multiplication of individuals in the same species.

ANSWER. It must be said that some have expressed themselves in different ways concerning this question:[4] For some have said that all

---

[3] In the French translation edited by S. Munk, I, p. 434.
[4] This question was not debated among the Latins before the coming in of Peripatetic philosophy. The Aristotelians, of course, Greeks as well as Arabs, all

spiritual substances belong to one species, but others, that all the angels of one hierarchy, or again, of one order, do. But others have said that all the angels differ from one another in species, and this seems to me also to be true, for three reasons.

The first reason is derived from the makeup of their substance. For it is necessary to say either that they are simple forms subsisting apart from matter, as was held above, or that they are forms that are composed of matter and form. Now if an angel is a simple form set apart from matter, it is impossible even to conceive several angels of one species; because any form whatever, however material and low, if it be set down as abstract either in actual being or in the intellect, remains but one form in one species.[5] For let "whiteness" be understood as something subsisting apart from every subject and it will not be possible to posit many whitenesses, since we see that "this whiteness" does not differ from "that whiteness" save through the fact that it is in this or in that subject. In similar fashion, if there were an abstract "human nature", there would be but one only. But if an angel is a substance that is composed of matter and form, it is necessary to say that the matters of different angels are somehow distinct. Now the distinction of matter from matter is found to be one of only two kinds: one according to the proper character of matter, and this is according to its relationship (habitudo) to different acts: for, since matter according to its proper character is in potency, whereas potency is spoken of in relation to act, a distinction among potencies and matters is made from the standpoint of the order of acts. And in this way the matter of lower bodies, which is a potency to actual being, differs from the matter of the heavenly bodies, which is a potency to place. The second distinction of matter, however, is based on quantitative division, inasmuch as matter which exists under these particular dimensions is distinguished from that which is under other dimensions. And the first distinction of matter causes a generic diversity[6] because, accord-

---

maintained that separated substances are not multiplied within one species; and so did the Latin Averroists. But I do not know whether any theologian before St. Thomas taught this doctrine clearly and consistently about the angels. Albert (*In II Sent.*, d. 9, a. 7), after saying that certain philosophers held that "all angels differ in species, and this seems to me more probable," goes on defending the contrary view, "that all are in one species," because it is "the more common opinion among the doctors."

5 Compare *In II Sent.*, d. 3, q. 1, a. 4, resp. and *Summa Theol.* I, q. 50, a. 4: "Yet if angels had matter, even then there could not be many angels of one species. For thus the principle of distinction of one from another would have to be matter, not indeed by way of a division of quantity, since they are incorporeal, but by way of a diversity of potencies; and such a diversity of matter causes a diversity not only of species but also of genus."

6 In this sentence alone is contained the fundamental argument of St. Thomas. In those which follow he rather tries to turn against his adversaries those arguments which they were accustomed to urge in behalf of the contrary view. Many weighty authors have believed that St. Thomas concedes the possibility of a multiplication

[90]

ing to the Philosopher in' V *Metaphysica* [28, 1024b 10], different things are generically different on a basis of matter. The second distinction of matter, however, causes a diversity of individuals within the same species. Now this second distinction of matter cannot exist among different angels, since angels are incorporeal and entirely without quantitative dimensions. The only remaining alternative, therefore, is that if there be many angels that are composed of matter and form, there is a distinction of matters among them according to the first mode: and thus it follows that they differ not only specifically but also generically.

The second reason is derived from the order of the universe. For it is obvious that the good of the universe is of two kinds: something that is separate, namely, God, Who is, as it were, the leader in an army; and a certain something in things themselves, and this is the order of the parts of the universe, just as the order of the parts of the army is the good of the army. Hence the Apostle says in *Romans* XIII [1]: "The things which are from God are ordered." Now the higher parts of the universe must have a greater share in the good of the universe, which is order. But those things in which there is order of themselves have a more perfect share in order than do those in which there is order only accidentally. Now it is obvious that among all the individuals of one species there is no order except accidentally: for they agree in the nature of the species and differ according to individuating principles and different accidents, which are related in an accidental way to the nature of the species. But things which differ in species have order of themselves and on a basis of their essential principles. For among the species of things, one is found to be greater than another, as is also the case in the species of numbers, as is said in VIII *Metaphysica* [3, 1043b 36].[7] However, in the case of those lower things which are subject to generation and corruption and make up the lowest part of the universe and have a lesser share in order, not all different things are found to have order of themselves, but certain ones have order only accidentally as, for example, the individuals of one species. But in the higher part of the universe, namely, among the heavenly bodies, order is not found accidentally but only essentially, since all heavenly bodies differ from one another in species, and there are not among them several individuals of one species, but one sun only, and one moon, and so of the others. Much more so, therefore, in the highest part of the universe there are not to be found

---

of angels in one species by a miracle, in a passage of *De Unitate Intellectus* (5, §105); but elsewhere I have shown that his apparent stand is due in great part to the corrupt text *(De Unit. Intell., ed. critica,* Rome 1936, *ad loc.).* Concerning *Quodl.* II, a. 4, see above, Art. 5, n. 12.

[7] Compare Arist., *Met.* XII, c. 10, 1075a 12.

any beings that are ordered accidentally and not essentially. And so the only remaining alternative is that all angels differ from one another in species, according to a greater and a less perfection of simple forms, as a result of a greater or a less nearness to God, Who is pure act and of infinite perfection.

But the third reason is derived from the perfection of the angelic nature. For each individual thing is said to be perfect when it lacks none of those things which pertain to it. And in fact the degree of this perfection can be calculated from the extremes of things. For to God, Who is at the apex of perfection, none of the things which belong to the character of actual being as a whole is lacking; for He has beforehand in Himself absolutely and in the highest degree all the perfections of things, as Dionysius says [De Divinis Nominibus, V, lec. 1]. But an individual in the lowest part of the world which contains beings that are subject to generation and corruption is found to be perfect from the fact that it has whatever pertains to itself, according to its own individual character, but not whatever pertains to its own specific nature, since its own specific nature is also found in other individual beings. And this quite obviously pertains to imperfection, not only in the case of animals that are subject to generation, among which one animal needs another of its own species for common life, but also in the case of all animals that are generated in any way whatever from semen, in which the male needs the female of its own species in order to generate; and further, in the case of all beings that are subject to generation and corruption, wherein a group of individuals of one species is necessary in order that the specific nature, which cannot be perpetually conserved in one individual being because of its corruptibility, may be conserved in many. But in the higher part of the universe a higher degree of perfection is found, wherein one individual being, such as the sun, is so perfect that it lacks none of the things that pertain to its own species, and hence also the whole matter of the species is contained in one individual being; and the same is true of the other heavenly bodies. Much more so, therefore, this perfection is found in the highest part of created things which is nearest to God, namely, among the angels: that one individual lacks none of the things which pertain to a whole species, and thus there are not several individuals in one species. But God, Who is at the summit of perfection, does not agree with any other being, not only in species but not even in genus, nor in any other univocal predicate.

As to the first argument, therefore, it must be said that Augustine is there speaking of angelic and human nature, not according as they are considered in their natural actual being, but according as they are ordered toward beatitude; for in this sense some in the angelic and in the human nature have perished. As for the order of beatitude, human nature is contrasted with the whole angelic nature, because the whole angelic nature is naturally such as has been produced to attain to beatitude or to fall short of it in one single way, irreparably, namely, right at the first choice; but human nature, in the course of time. And consequently, Augustine is speaking there of all angels as of one nature, by reason of the single mode of their relation to beatitude, although they are different in the species of that nature.

As to the second, it must be said that whenever one inquires into specific difference or similarity, things are being studied from the standpoint of their natures. And on this basis, one must not speak of all angels as of one nature that is closest to God, but only the first angel was, from this point of view, the nature closest to God. And in this nature there is the least possible diversity, because there is neither specific nor numerical diversity.

As to the third, it must be said that actual being itself is related as an act, both to composite natures and to simple natures. Therefore, just as in the case of composite natures the species is not derived from their actual being itself, but from their form, because a species is predicated as something essential, whereas actual being seems to pertain to the question of a thing's existence; and hence, neither in the case of angelic substances is the species obtained on a basis of actual being itself, but on a basis of simple subsistent forms, whose difference depends on the order of perfection, as has been said.

As to the fourth, it must be said that just as a form, which is in a subject or in matter, is individuated by the fact that it is in this particular thing, so a separated form is individuated by the fact that it is not naturally such as to exist in anything. For, just as actually being in this particular thing excludes the commonness of a universal, which is predicated of many individuals, so does not being able to exist in some subject. Accordingly, just as "this particular whiteness" is not prevented from having many individuals under it in consequence of the fact that it is whiteness, which pertains to its specific character, but in consequence of the fact that it is in "this particular subject", which pertains to its individual character, so the nature of "this particular angel" is not prevented from existing in many in consequence of the fact that it is a nature in a given order of things, which pertains to its specific character, but in consequence of the fact that this nature has not a natural capacity for being received in a given subject, which pertains to the character of an individual.

As to the fifth, it must be said that, since affection follows knowledge, the more universal knowledge is, so much the more does the affection which follows it look toward the common good; and the more particular the knowledge is, so much the more does the affection which follows it look toward a private good; and hence among us too, individual love arises as a consequence of sense knowledge, but the love of the common and absolute good arises as a consequence of intellectual knowledge. Accordingly, because the angels, in proportion as they are higher, possess a more universal knowledge, as Dionysius says in the twelfth chapter of *De Caelesti Hierarchia* [§2, *PG* I, 298], so does their love, as a consequence, look especially to the common good. Consequently they love one another more if they differ in species, which pertains rather to the perfection of the universe, as has been shown, than if they were to agree in species, which would pertain to the private good of a single species.

As to the sixth, it must be said that our soul when it is united to the body cannot understand separated substances in their essences, so as to know of them what they are; because their essences are above the genus of sensible natures and out of proportion to them, and from these our intellect gets its knowledge. And consequently separated substances cannot be defined by us in the strict sense, but only through negation or through some activity of these same substances. And in this way Damascene defines an angel, not by a definition belonging to the most specific species, but to a subordinate genus, which is a genus and a species, and hence a definition is possible.

As to the seventh, it must be said that the mode of distinction between the divine persons is unconnected with diversity of essence, and this a created nature does not allow; and consequently this fact cannot lead to a conclusion in the case of creatures.

As to the eighth, it must be said that "more and less" is taken in two senses; in one sense, with reference to a different manner of participating in one and the same form, just as a more white thing is said to be more bright than a less white thing, and in this sense "more and less" do not constitute a specific difference. In another sense, "more and less" is used with reference to a degree of different forms; thus, for instance, something white is said to be more bright than red or green; and in this sense "more and less" do constitute a specific difference; and in this way angels differ in natural spiritual gifts on a basis of "more and less".

As to the ninth, it must be said that what establishes something in a species is more noble than what establishes something in a genus, in the sense in which something determinate is more noble than something indeterminate; for the determinate is related to the indeterminate as act is related to potency; not, however, in the sense that what establishes something in a species always belongs to a more noble nature, as is evident in the species of irrational animals: for species of this sort are not constituted by the addition of another more noble nature over and above the sentient nature, which is the noblest nature in them, but through their being determined to different degrees within that nature. And something similar must be said of the intellectual nature, which is the common characteristic in angels.

As to the tenth, it must be said that it does not seem to be universally true that a more imperfect generic difference is multiplied into several species. For "body" is divided into "animate body" and "inanimate body"; yet there would seem to be more species of animate bodies than of inanimate, particularly if the heavenly bodies are animate, and if all the stars differ from one another in species. But both in plants and in animals there is a very great diversity of species. Still, in order that the truth of this matter may be investigated, it must be borne in mind that Dionysius would seem to present a view that is contrary to the Platonists. For the Platonists say that the nearer substances are to the primary one, the less numerous they are. But Dionysius says in the fourteenth chapter of *De Caelesti Hierarchia* [*PG* I, 322] that angels transcend all material manyness. Now, that both these statements are true, anyone can perceive from corporeal objects, among which the higher a given body is found to be, the less matter it has, but the greater is its quantitative extent. And hence, since number is, in a way, the cause of continuous quantity, seeing that unity constitutes a point and a point constitutes a line (speaking after the fashion of the Platonists), so also is it the case in the whole universe that the higher some things are among beings, the more do they have of formal manyness, which is reckoned according to a distinction of species, and in this sense the saying of Dionysius is saved; whereas they have less of material manyness, which is reckoned according to a distinction between individuals within the same species: and in this sense the saying of the Platonists is saved. Now the fact that there is only one species of rational animal, although many species of irrational animals exist, arises from the fact that "rational animal" is constituted on this basis: that corporeal nature at its highest point touches the nature of spiritual substances at its lowest point. Now the highest level of any nature, or even the lowest level, is one only. Although it might be said that there are many species of rational animals, if one were to hold that the heavenly bodies are animate.

As to the eleventh, it must be said that men are included among corruptible creatures, which form the lowest part of the universe, wherein are found some beings that are related not only essentially, but also accidentally. And consequently in the church militant, a difference in power and in orders does not make a difference of species; but it is otherwise in the case of the angels, who form the highest part of the

[95]

universe, as has been said. Now there is in men a likeness to angels, although not a perfect likeness, but one that is accidental, as has been said.

As to the twelfth, it must be said that the ornaments of earth and of water, because they are corruptible, need manyness within the same species, as has been said. Now the heavenly bodies also are of different species, as has been said. For light is not their substantial form, since it is a directly sensible quality, and this cannot be said of any substantial form; and furthermore, light does not have the same character in all things, as is clear from the fact that the radiations of different bodies have different effects.

As to the thirteenth, it must be said that individuation in the case of the angels is not through matter, but through the fact that they are self-subsistent forms, which do not have a natural capacity for existing in a subject or in matter, as has been said.

As to the fourteenth, it must be said that the early philosophers asserted that the knowing subject should be of the same nature as the thing known. Hence Empedocles [Aristotle, I *De An.*, 2, 404b 13] said that "We know the earth through earth and the water through water." But to rule this out, Aristotle [III *De An.*, 4, 429a 21] asserted that the knowing power in us, according as it is in potency, is void of the nature of the things that can be known; thus, the pupil of the eye, for instance, is void of color. But yet the sense in act is the thing sensed in act, inasmuch as the sense is put in act through being informed by the sensible species; and by the same reasoning the intellect in act is the thing understood in act, inasmuch as it is informed by the intelligible species: "for a stone does not exist in the soul, but the species of a stone", as he himself says [III *De An.*, 8, 431b 29]. Now the reason why something is intelligible in act is that it is separated from matter; and consequently he says [III *De An.*, 4, 430a 2] that "In those things which are without matter, the understanding subject and the thing which is understood are the same." Therefore the understanding angel need not be the same in substance as the understood angel, if they are immaterial; but the understanding of the one must be informed by a likeness of the other.[8]

As to the fifteenth, it must be said that the number which is caused by the division of a continuum is a species of quantity, and it exists only in material substances. But in immaterial substances there is a many-ness which derives from the transcendentals, inasmuch as "one" and

---

[8] Compare the long question *De Ver.* VIII, 7: "Does one angel understand another?"

"many" are divisions of being; and this manyness is the result of a formal distinction.[9]

As to the sixteenth, it must be said that a difference of cause and effect is asserted by some to multiply separated substances, inasmuch as they assert that different degrees arise among them, insofar as an effect is lower than its cause. Hence if we assert different degrees among spiritual substances in consequence of the arrangement of the divine wisdom which is their cause, the character of the distinction will remain the same, even though one of these substances is not the cause of the other.

As to the seventeenth, it must be said that no created nature, since it is finite, represents the divine goodness as perfectly as a multitude of natures does, because what is contained in many natures in a multiple way is included in God as a unit; and consequently there ought to be many natures in the universe, and also among the angelic substances.

As to the eighteenth, it must be said that the opposition of the differences that constitute the angelic species is understood on a basis of perfect and imperfect, or the exceeding and the exceeded; as is the case also in numbers; and thus also, animate is related to inanimate, and other things of the sort.

---

[9] How immaterial substances can exist and how they are numerically many is more fully explained in De Unit. Intell. 5, §§101-103, 107.

THE ninth question is: Is the possible intellect one in all men?[1] ᴺᴼ

And it would seem that it is. *1* For Augustine says in the book *De Quantitate Animae* [XXXII, 69, *PL* XXXII, 1073]: "If ever I say that there are many souls, I shall be smiling at myself." It seems laughable, therefore, to say that there are many intellectual souls.

2 Furthermore, in those things which are without matter, there is one individual in one species, as has been shown [Art. VIII]. But the possible intellect, or the intellectual soul, since it is a spiritual substance, is not composed of matter and form, as was shown before [Art. I]. Therefore there is only one intellectual soul, or possible intellect, in the whole human species.

But the objector said that even if the intellectual soul does not have matter of which it is made, nevertheless it has matter in which it exists, namely, the body, and in consequence of the multiplication of these intellectual souls are multiplied. But on the other hand *3*, when the cause is removed the effect is removed. If, then, the multiplication of bodies is the cause of the multiplication of souls, when the bodies are removed a multiplicity of souls cannot remain.

4 Furthermore, individuation takes place by way of a determination of essential principles: for, just as it is of the essence of man to be composed of a soul and a body, so it is of the essence of Socrates to be composed of "this particular soul" and "this particular body", as is clear from the Philosopher in VII *Metaphysica* [10, 1035b 29]. But the body is not of the essence of the soul. Therefore it is impossible for a soul to be individuated by a body, and so souls will not be multiplied in consequence of the multiplication of bodies.

5 Furthermore, Augustine[2] says in *Contra Felicianum* [XII, *PL* XLII, 1167]: "If we seek the origin of the power of a living thing, the soul is prior to the mother, and it seems to have been born of her again along with the offspring," and he is speaking of "the soul by which the mother is animated," as he immediately adds. From this he seems

---

[1] *In II Sent.*, d. 17, q. 2, a. 1; *Contra Gentiles* II, cap. 59, 73, 75; *Summa Theol.* I, q. 76, a. 1-2; *Q. De An.* 2-3*; *In De An.* III, lec. 7 (689-699) and 8 (719); *De Unitate Intell.**, cc. 4-5; *Compend. Theol.*, 85.
    Aristotle, *De An.* III, c. 4. Avicenna, *De An.*, c. 3. Algazel, *De An.* II, tr. 4, c. 5. Averroes, *In III De An.*, comm. 4-8 and 36. Guil. Alvernus, *De Universo* II, 1, cc. 10-11 (p. 817); *De An.* VII, cc. 3-4. Albertus M., *Summa de Creat.* II, 1, q. 2, a. 5 and q. 3, a. 2, vol. 35, pp. 17 and 29; *In III De An.*, tr. 2, c. 7, vol. 5, p. 340; *Opusc. De Unit. Intell.*, vol. 9, p. 437 (almost the same as in *Summa Theol.* II, q. 77, vol. 33, p. 75). St. Bonaventure, *In II Sent.*, d. 18, a. 2, q. 1, p. 446. *Summa Philos.*, tr. II, c. 10 (briefly at the end). Roger Bacon, *Comm. Nat.* IV, 3, c. 3, pp. 286-291. (Among the outstanding Peripatetics only Averroes asserted that the possible intellect too is one and separate.)
[2] The true author is thought to have been Vigilius Tapsensis.

to say that there is the same soul in the mother and in the son, and for the same reason in all men.

6 Furthermore, if the possible intellect were one thing in me and another in you, the thing that is understood would have to be one thing in me and another in you, since the thing that is understood is in the intellect; and thus the thing that is understood would have to be counted by counting individual men. But all things which are counted by counting individuals have in common a thing that is understood; and thus for a thing that is understood there will be a thing that is understood, and on to infinity,[3] which is impossible. Therefore there is not one possible intellect in me and another in you.

7 Furthermore, if there were not one possible intellect in all men, whenever it happens that knowledge is caused in a pupil by a teacher it would have to be the case that either the numerically same knowledge which is in the teacher would flow into the pupil, or that the knowledge of the teacher would cause the knowledge of the pupil as the heat of fire causes heat in faggots,[4] or else learning would be nothing but remembering. For if a pupil has the knowledge that he learns before he learns it, learning is remembering. But if he does not have it previously, either he acquires it as something that exists previously in another, namely, in the teacher; or as something that does not exist previously in another; and in that case it would have to be caused in him anew by another. Now these three things are impossible. For, since knowledge is an accident, the numerically same knowledge cannot pass over from subject to subject, because, as Boethius says [In Categ. I, PL LXIV, 173], accidents can be corrupted but they cannot be transmuted. Similarly, also, it is impossible for the knowledge of the teacher to cause knowledge in the pupil, not only because knowledge is not an active quality but also because the words which the teacher utters only stimulate the pupil to understanding, as Augustine says in the book De Magistro [passim]. Moreover, the statement that learning is remembering is contrary to the Philosopher in I Posteriora [1, 71a]. Therefore, there are not different possible intellects in all men.

8 Furthermore, every cognitive power which is in corporeal matter knows only those things which have an affinity with the matter in which it is; thus, for instance, the sight knows only colors, which have

---

[3] According to the statement of Averroes (In III De An., comm. 5, f. 166r): "And thus the thing that is understood will possess a thing that is understood, and so there is an infinite process." Cf. below, obj. 13.
[4] "Thus," says Averroes (In III De An., comm. 5), "it will be impossible for the pupil to learn from the master, unless the knowledge which is in the master is a power that creates and generates the knowledge which is in the pupil, in the manner in which fire generates another fire like to itself in species; which is impossible."

an affinity with the pupil, which is able to take on colors because of its own transparency. But the possible intellect is not able to take on only those things which have an affinity either with the whole body or with some part of it. Therefore, the possible intellect is not a cognitive power in corporeal matter, neither in the whole body nor in any part of it. Therefore it is not multiplied in consequence of the multiplication of bodies.

9 Furthermore, if the intellectual soul or the possible intellect is multiplied in consequence of the multiplication of bodies, this is the case only because it is the form of the body. But it cannot be the form of the body, since it is composed of matter and form [it cannot be the form of anything],[5] as many assert; for a thing that is composed of matter and form cannot be the form of anything. Therefore the intellectual soul or the possible intellect cannot be multiplied in consequence of the multiplication of bodies.

10 Furthermore, as Cyprian says [*Epist. ad Magnum, PL* III, 1143], the Lord forbade his disciples to enter the city of the Samaritans because of the sin of schism, — because the ten tribes had seceded from the kingdom of David, afterwards establishing a sovereign kingdom for themselves in Samaria. Now it was the same people in the time of Christ as it had previously been. Now a people is to a people as a man is to a man and a soul is to a soul. Therefore, by the same reasoning one soul is in him who lived formerly and in another who follows after; and so through the same reasoning the same soul will be in each individual man.

11 Furthermore, an accident depends on its subject more than a form depends on its matter, since the form gives actual being to the matter absolutely, whereas an accident does not give actual being to a subject absolutely. But one accident can exist in many subjects, just as there is one time in many movements, as Anselm says [*Dialogus de veritate,* fin., *PL* CLVIII, 486]. Therefore much more can one soul belong to many bodies, and thus there do not have to be many possible intellects.

12 Furthermore, the intellectual soul is more powerful than the vegetative. But the vegetative soul is able to quicken something outside the body whose form it is; for Augustine says in VI *De Musica* [VIII, 21] that the sight rays[6] are quickened by the soul of the one who sees, and are even projected far out to the thing that is seen. Therefore

---

[5] The words within brackets [ ] were evidently taken by the scribe from the following line by mistake; and yet they are present in all our manuscripts.
[6] According to Augustine the eyes send forth rays of light, through the medium of which things are seen by the soul.

much more can the intellectual soul perfect other bodies in addition to the body wherein it is.

13 Furthermore,[7] if the possible intellect is multiplied in consequence of the multiplication of bodies, the intelligible species, which are in the possible intellect in me and in you, must be multiplied in consequence of the multiplication of bodies. But from all forms that are multiplied in consequence of the multiplication of corporeal matter there can be abstracted some common notion. Therefore from the forms that are understood through the possible intellect there can be abstracted some common notion that is understood; and by the same reasoning, since that understood notion is multiplied in consequence of the multiplication of the possible intellect, there will be an abstracting of another understood notion, on to infinity. Now this is impossible. There is, then, one possible intellect in all men.

14 Furthermore, all men agree on first principles. But this would not be the case if that whereby they know first principles were not one thing common in all men. Now such is the possible intellect. There is, then, one possible intellect in all men.

15 Furthermore, no form that is individuated and multiplied through matter is understood in act. But the possible intellect, whenever it actually understands, is the intellect in act; and the intellect in act is the thing that is understood in act, as is said in III *De Anima* [7, 431a 1]. just as the sense in act is the thing that is sensed in act. Therefore the possible intellect is not individuated nor multiplied through corporeal matter; and so it is one in all men.

16 Furthermore, a thing that is received is in the recipient according to the mode of the recipient. But an intelligible species is received in the intellect as something understood in act and not individuated by matter; therefore neither is it multiplied by the multiplication of corporeal matter.

17 Furthermore, the possible intellect even of Socrates or of Plato understands its own essence, since the intellect reflects on itself; therefore the very essence of the possible intellect is understood in act. But no form that is individuated and multiplied by matter is understood in act. Therefore the possible intellect is not individuated and multiplied by corporeal matter; and thus the only remaining alternative is that there is one possible intellect in all men.

But on the other hand *i* there is what is said in *Apocalypse* VII [9]: "After this I saw a great multitude, which no man could number." Now that multitude was not composed of men living in a bodily way, but of souls set free from the body. Therefore there are many intellec-

---

[7] This is the same objection as the sixth above.

[handwritten annotations at top: possible intellect — doesn't have in own nature essence any sensible but is in potency to all things / agent intellect — abstracts species things from matter + individuating conditions]

tual souls, not only now, merely when they are united to the body, but also when they are set free from bodies.

ii Furthermore, Augustine[8] says in *Contra Felicianum* [XII, *PL* XLII, 1166, 1167]: "Let us imagine, as many wish, that there is a universal soul in the world"; and afterwards he adds: "When we propose such things, let us say in advance that they are objectionable." Therefore it is unlikely that there is one soul belonging to all men.

iii Furthermore, the intellectual soul is more closely bound to the human body than its mover is to a heavenly body. But the Commentator says in III *De Anima* [cf. comm. 5, f. 166r] that if there were several movable bodies there would be several movers in the heavenly spheres. All the more, therefore, since there are many human bodies, will there be many intellectual souls, and not just one possible intellect.

ANSWER. It must be said that to make this question clear it is necessary to understand in advance what is meant by the term "possible intellect" and "agent intellect". Now it must be noted that Aristotle [III, 4, 429a 13] went on to a study of the intellect by way of a comparison with the senses. Now as regards the senses, since we find ourselves sometimes sensing in potency and sometimes in act, it is necessary to posit in us some sense power whereby we may be sensing in potency, and this power must be in potency to the species of sensible things, and not have any of these species actually in its own essence; otherwise, if the senses were to possess sensible things in act, as the ancient philosophers asserted, it would follow that we would always be sensing in act. Similarly, since we find ourselves sometimes understanding in act and sometimes in potency, it is necessary to posit some power whereby we may be understanding in potency, and this power does not have in its own essence and nature any of the natures of sensible things which we can understand, but it should be in potency to all things; and on this account it is called the possible intellect; just as the sense power too, according as it is in potency, might be called the "possible sense." Now a sense which is in potency is reduced to act through objects that are actually sensible, which are outside the soul, and hence it is not necessary to posit an agent sense. And similarly it would not be necessary to posit an agent intellect if the universals which are actually intelligible subsisted of themselves outside the soul, as Plato asserted. But because Aristotle asserted that these universals do not subsist except in sensible objects, which are not actually intelligible, he necessarily had to posit some power, which would make the objects that are intelligible in potency to be actually intelligible, by abstracting the species

---

[8] Vigilius Tapsensis.

of things from matter and from individuating conditions; and this power is called the agent intellect.

Concerning the possible intellect, Averroes in *Commentum III De Anima* [comm. f. 164] asserted that there was a kind of substance existentially separated from the bodies of men, but that it was connected with us through phantasms;[9] and secondly, that there was one possible intellect for all. [Now that this assertion is contrary to faith is easy to see: for it takes away the rewards and punishments of a future life.] But it must be shown that this assertion is in itself impossible[10] according to the true principles of philosophy. Now it was shown above [Art. II] when we were discussing the union of a spiritual substance with a body that on this view it would follow that no particular man would understand anything. But granted, for the sake of argument, that some particular man would be able to understand through an intellect that is so separated, three incongruities follow if it be asserted that there is one possible intellect for all men, whereby they all understand.

(1) The first is that it is not possible for one power to have many actions at one and the same time with respect to the same subject. Now it happens that two men at one and the same time may understand one and the same intelligible thing. If, then, they both understand through one possible intellect, it would follow that they both have numerically one and the same intellectual activity; thus, for instance, if two men were to see by means of a single eye, it would follow that the same act of seeing belongs to both. It is clear that this is utterly impossible. Nor can it be said that my act of understanding is different from your act of understanding by reason of the diversity of the phantasms; because a phantasm is not a thing that is understood in act, but this latter is something abstracted from it, which is held to be a word. Hence the diversity of the phantasms is extrinsic to intellectual activity, and thus cannot cause differences in it.[11]

(2) The second is that it is impossible for that whereby individuals obtain their species to be numerically one in the individuals of the same species. For if two horses should agree in that numerically same reality whereby they obtained their species "horse", it would follow that two

---

[9] How that connection is made according to Averroes, St. Thomas explained above (Art. 2, resp.).

[10] This difficulty is repeatedly urged by St. Thomas (*Q. De An.* 3, resp.; *De Unit. Intell.* 4, §§90-91). And it is cited again by Siger of Brabant (*De Anima Intellectiva*, q. 7) among those arguments which to him cast doubt on the single intellect for all men.

[11] Compare *De Unit. Intell.* 5, §91: "For phantasms are preliminary to the action of the intellect, as colors are to the action of seeing; and hence through their diversity the action of the intellect could not be diversified, especially in regard to some one intelligible."

horses are one horse, which is impossible. And on this account it is said in VII *Metaphysica* [10, 1035b 30] that the principles of a species, once they are determinate, constitute an individual: thus, if the essence of man is that he be composed of soul and body, it is of the essence of "this man" that he be composed of "this soul" and "this body". Hence the principles of every species must be multiplied in the several individuals of the same species. Now that from which a thing obtains its species is known through some proper activity that is a consequence of the species. For we judge that to be true gold which has the proper activity of gold. Now the proper activity of the human species is understanding; and hence, in accordance with this activity the Philosopher in X *Ethica* [7] sets forth the ultimate happiness of man. Now the principle of this activity is not the passive intellect,[12] that is, the cogitative power or the sense-appetite which somehow participates in reason, since these powers have no activity except through a corporeal organ; whereas the act of understanding cannot take place through a corporeal organ, as is proven in III *De Anima* [4]. And thus the only remaining alternative is that the possible intellect is that whereby this particular man obtains his human species, and not the passive intellect, as Averroes imagines [*In* III *De An.*, comm. 20]. The only remaining alternative, therefore, is that it is impossible that there be one possible intellect in all men.

Thirdly, it would follow that the possible intellect would not receive any species that are abstracted from our phantasms, if one intellect belongs to all those who are and who have been. Because, now that many men who knew many things have already gone before us, it would follow that with respect to all those things which they knew the possible intellect would be in act and not in potency to receive them, because nothing receives what it already has.[13] And from this it would further follow that if we are made understanding and knowing through the possible intellect, knowing in our case is nothing but remembering. And yet too this very thing in itself would seem incongruous: that the possible intellect if it be an existentially separated substance should be reduced to act through the phantasms, since the higher things among beings do not need lower things for their own

---

12 Many commentators have distinguished the passive intellect from the intellect in potency, or the possible intellect, on the ground that Aristotle in III *De An.* after having said (c. 4) that this latter is unmixed and separable, declared that the passive intellect (c. 5) is corruptible. Cf. St. Thomas *In* III *De An.*, lec. 10, 745.

13 Compare *De Unit. Intell.* 5, §94: "If, therefore, through any of the preceding men one intellect has been actuated as regards some intelligible species and has been perfected by a habit of knowledge, that habit and those species remain in it. Now, since every thing that receives is void of that which it is receiving, it is impossible that those species are acquired in the possible intellect by my act of learning or remembering."

perfection. For just as it would be incongruous to say that heavenly bodies are perfected in act by receiving something from lower bodies, similarly (and all the more so) it is impossible for a separated substance to be perfected in act by receiving something from phantasms.

It is also obvious that this assertion is opposed to the words of Aristotle.[14] For when he begins his investigation of the possible intellect, right from the beginning he calls it a "part of the soul", saying [III *De An.*, 4, 429a 10] : "Now about the part of the soul whereby the soul knows and perceives." But when he wishes to investigate the nature of the possible intellect, he first states a difficulty, namely, whether the intellectual part is separable from the other parts of the soul as a subsistent thing, as Plato asserted, or mentally only; and this is what he says [429a 11] : "Whether it be separable as an existing thing or inseparable spatially but mentally." From this it is clear that whichever of these assertions is made, the opinion which he had in mind concerning the possible intellect will still hold good.[15] But it would not hold good that the possible intellect is separated only mentally, if the assertion that was mentioned before were a true one. Hence the opinion that was mentioned before is not the view of Aristotle. Afterwards he also adds [429a 23] that the possible intellect is "that whereby the soul forms opinions and understands", and many other things of this kind; and from these statements he manifestly gives us to understand that the possible intellect is something belonging to the soul and is not a separated substance.

As to the first argument, therefore, it must be said that Augustine means that it is laughable that many souls are asserted to belong to different men, only in this sense, that they differ in number and in species; and especially from the point of view of the Platonists, who have posited some one general subsisting being above all the things which belong to one species.

As to the second, it must be said that the angels, just as they possess no matter of which they are made, so they do not possess matter in which they exist; but the soul has matter in which it exists, and consequently the angels cannot be many in one species, but souls can be many of one species.

As to the third, it must be said that as the body is related to the soul's actual being, so it is to its individuation, because each individual thing is both one and a being on the same basis. Now a soul's actual being accrues to it in consequence of its being united to a body with which

---

[14] Throughout the entire first chapter of *De Unit. Intell.* the true mind of Aristotle is explored.

[15] In other words, in that passage Aristotle so sets forth his view on the possible intellect that it is valid in both hypotheses, whether the possible intellect be separated or not; therefore he does not suppose an Averroistic doctrine.

it simultaneously constitutes one nature, whereof both are a part. And yet, because the intellectual soul is a form that transcends the capacity of the body, it possesses an actual being of its own on a higher level than the body; and hence after the body has been destroyed, the soul's actual being still remains. And similarly, souls are multiplied along with bodies, and yet when the bodies have been removed, a multiplicity of souls still remains.

As to the fourth, it must be said that although the body is not of the essence of the soul, yet the soul because of its own essence has a relation to the body, inasmuch as it is essential for it to be the form of a body; and accordingly body is set down in the definition of the soul. Just as, accordingly, it is essential to the soul that it be the form of a body, so it is essential to "this soul", insofar as it is "this soul", that it have a relation to "this body."

As to the fifth, it must be said that Augustine's statement in that passage is based on the opinion of those who assert that there is one universal soul, as is clear from the preceding context.

As to the sixth, it must be said that Averroes seems to lay special stress on this argument [*In* III *De An.*, comm. 5, f. 166], because it would follow, as he himself says, that if the possible intellect were not one in all men the thing that is understood would be individuated and counted by means of the individuation and counting of individual men; and thus it would be understood potentially and not in act. It must accordingly be shown that, first, those incongruities follow no less for those who assert that there is one possible intellect than for those who assert that it is multiplied in many. And first of all as regards individuation, it is obvious that a form that exists in some individual is individuated by that individual in the same way, whether it be the only individual in some one species, like the sun, or whether there be many in one species, like pearls: for in both cases the species "brightness" is individuated. For one must say that the possible intellect is a kind of singular individual thing; for acts belong to individuals. Whether, then, it is one in one species, or many, the thing that is understood will be individuated in it in the same way. But as regards multiplication, it is obvious that if there are not many possible intellects in the human species, there are nevertheless many intellects in the universe, and many of them understand one and the same thing. The same difficulty, therefore, will remain whether the thing that is understood is one or many in different men. Therefore it is not possible to prove his point by this means, because even after this stand has been taken, the same incongruities will still remain.

And consequently, for the solution of this problem it must be borne in mind that if we have to speak of the intellect by way of a comparison

[106]

with the senses, as is clear from the procedure of Aristotle in III *De Anima*, we must say that the thing which is understood is not related to the possible intellect as an intelligible species whereby the possible intellect is actuated, but that species is as a formal principle whereby the intellect understands. Now that which is understood, or the thing which is understood,[16] is as something which is constituted or formed through the activity of the intellect, whether this thing be a simple quiddity or whether it be the composition and division of a proposition. For Aristotle specifies these two activities of the intellect in III *De Anima* [6], — the one activity, namely, which he calls "the understanding of indivisible things", whereby the intellect apprehends the essence of a given thing, and this the Arabs call "formation" or "imagination by the intellect",[17] but he posits another activity, namely, the combining and separating of concepts, which the Arabs call "belief" or "faith". Now for both of these activities an intelligible species is presupposed, whereby the possible intellect is actuated; because the possible intellect does not act except according as it is in act, just as the sight does not see except through being actuated by a species which makes seeing possible. And hence the species which makes seeing possible is not as a thing which is seen, but as that whereby the object is seen. And the same is true of the possible intellect, except that the possible intellect reflects upon itself and upon its own species, whereas the sight does not.

Accordingly, a thing that is understood by two intellects is in a way one and the same thing, and in a way it is many things: because on the part of the object which is known it is one and the same thing; but on the part of the knowledge itself it is two different things. Thus, for instance, if two persons should see one wall, it is the same thing which is seen so far as the thing which is seen is concerned, yet it is two different things from the standpoint of the different acts of seeing; and there would be something exactly like this on the part of the intellect, if the thing which is understood subsisted outside the soul as does the thing which is seen, as the Platonists asserted. But according to the view of Aristotle there seems to be a greater difficulty, although the explanation is the same if one looks into the matter rightly. For there is no difference between Aristotle and Plato, except in this: that Plato

---

[16] Here St. Thomas means the species that is expressed through the intellect or "the thing that is understood" of Averroes. Concerning this Roger Bacon says (*Comm. Nat.* IV, c. 3): "But many explain it in several ways, some as referring to the thing that is understood, and some as referring to the species of the thing in the mind." Compare the long discussion in *De Unit. Intell.* (5, §§109-112.)

[17] Algazel's *Logic* begins thus: of the sciences "there are two properties, imagination and belief. Imagination is the apprehension of the things which single words signify . . . But belief is like when one says: the world began to exist." But we must not believe, because of such terminology, that the Arabs conceived these acts differently from the rest of the Peripatetics.

asserted that the thing which is understood has actual being outside the soul in exactly the same way as the intellect understands it, that is, as something abstract and universal; but Aristotle asserted that the thing which is understood is outside the soul, but in another way, because it is understood in the abstract and has actual being in the concrete. And just as, according to Plato, the thing itself which is understood is outside the soul itself, so it is according to Aristotle: and this is clear from the fact that neither of them asserted that the sciences have to do with those things which are in our intellect, as with substances; but whereas Plato said that the sciences have to do with separated forms, Aristotle said that they have to do with the quiddities of things that exist in those things. But the character of universality, which consists in commonness and abstractness, is merely the result of the mode of understanding, inasmuch as we understand things abstractly and universally; but according to Plato it is also the result of the mode of existence of the abstract forms: and consequently Plato asserted that universals subsist, whereas Aristotle did not. Thus then it is clear how the plurality of intellects does not militate against the universality, nor the generality, nor the unity of the thing that is understood.

As to the seventh, it must be said that knowledge is caused by a teacher in a pupil, not as heat is caused in faggots by fire, but as health in a sick person by a doctor, who causes health inasmuch as he furnishes some remedies which nature makes use of to cause health; and consequently the doctor proceeds in the same order, in his curing, as nature would cure. For just as the principal healing force is one's interior nature, so the principle which chiefly causes knowledge is something intrinsic, namely, the light of the agent intellect, whereby knowledge is caused in us, when we descend through the application of universal principles to some special points, which we gain through experience in discovery. And similarly the teacher draws universal principles down to special conclusions; and hence Aristotle says in I *Posteriora* [2, 71b] that "a demonstration is a syllogism that causes knowledge."

As to the eighth, it must be said that in this reasoning Averroes also was deceived; for he thought that because Aristotle said that the possible intellect is something separate, it would be separated existentially, and as a consequence would not be multiplied in consequence of the multiplication of bodies. But Aristotle means that the possible intellect is a power of the soul, which is not an act of any organ, as though it were to have an activity of its own through some corporeal organ, just as the visual power is the power of an organ and has its activity through a corporeal organ. And because the possible intellect does not have its activity through a corporeal organ, it is consequently not necessary that it know only those things which have an affinity either with the whole body or with a part of the body.

As to the ninth, it must be said that the opinion which holds that the soul is composed of matter and form is entirely false and unprovable. For it could not be the form of the body if it were composed of matter and form. For if the soul were the form of the body in view of its own form only, it would follow that one and the same form would perfect the different kinds of matter of different genera, namely, the spiritual matter of the soul and corporeal matter; and this is impossible since a proper potency has its own proper act. And furthermore, that thing composed of matter and form would not be the soul, but the form of the soul. For whenever we say "soul" we mean that which is the form of the body. But if the form of the soul were the form of the body through the medium of its own matter, as color is an act of a body through the medium of the surface, so that in this way the whole soul could be called the form of the body, — this is impossible, because by "matter" we mean that which is in potency only; but what is in potency only cannot be the act of anything, that is, be a form. But if someone were to mean by the term "matter" a given act, we need not mind; because nothing prevents someone else from calling "matter" what we call "act"; just as, for instance, what we call "stone" someone else can call "ass".[18]

As to the tenth, it must be said that as the Seine river[19] is not "this particular river" because of "this flowing water", but because of "this source" and "this bed", and hence is always called the same river, although there may be other water flowing down it; likewise a people is the same, not because of a sameness of soul or of men, but because of the same dwelling place, or rather because of the same laws and the same manner of living, as Aristotle says in III *Politica* [1].

As to the eleventh, it must be said that time is related to one movement only as an accident is to a subject, namely, to the movement of the first movable thing by which all other movements are measured. Now to other movements time is related as a measure to a thing that is measured; so, for instance, an ell is related to a wooden rod as to a subject, but to a piece of cloth which is measured by it as to a thing that is measured only; and consequently it does not follow that one accident is in many subjects.

As to the twelfth, it must be said that seeing is not caused by rays that are sent out, as a matter of fact; but Augustine says this accord-

---

[18] Cf. Art. I, resp.
[19] In the Introduction we have already spoken of the importance of this remark in discussions concerning the year and the place where this question was composed.

ing to the opinion of others.[20] But supposing this to be true, the soul would quicken rays, however far they are sent out, not as foreign bodies, but insofar as they are connected with its own body.

As to the thirteenth, it must be said that, as is clear from what has been said above, a thing that is understood is not individuated nor multiplied except from the standpoint of intellectual activity. Now it is not incongruous that from a thing that is understood, insofar as it is understood, there is still abstracted a thing that is understood in an absolute sense, just as from "this particular understanding being", for instance, is abstracted "understanding" in an absolute sense. Nor does this militate against the character of universality. For it is accidental to man or to the concept "species", that it is understood by me; hence it is not essential to the understanding of man or the concept "species" that it be understood by me or by someone else.

As to the fourteenth, it must be said that agreement on first principles is not caused by a oneness of the possible intellect but by that likeness of nature in consequence of which we all are inclined toward the same thing; thus, for instance, all sheep agree in considering a wolf as an enemy; yet no one would say that there is only one soul in them.

As to the fifteenth, it must be said that "to be something individual" is not incompatible with "being understood in act": because separated substances are understood in act although they are nevertheless individual substances; otherwise they would not have actions, which belong to singular things. But "to have material being" is incompatible with "being understood in act"; and consequently individual forms which are individuated by matter are not understood in act, but in potency only. Now the intellectual soul is not so individuated by matter as to become a material form, especially in view of its intellect, in consequence of which it transcends its relationship to corporeal matter; but in this sense it is individuated on the basis of corporeal matter, as has been said, namely, inasmuch as it has an aptitude for being the form of "this particular body". And hence it is not thereby impossible for the possible intellect of "this particular man" to be understood in act, and the same applies to those things which are received in the intellect.

And through this the solution to the two following arguments is clear.

---

[20] This also seems to be the opinion of Augustine himself; cf. *De Quant. Animae* XXIII, 43; *De Gen. ad Litt.* I, xvi, 31; *ibid.* IV, xxiv, 54; *De Trin.* IX, iii, 3.

Article X

THE tenth question is: Is the agent intellect one intellect belonging to all men?[1] NO

And it would seem that it is.[2] *1* For to enlighten men is proper to God, according to that passage in *John* I [9]: "That was the true light which enlighteneth" and so on. But this pertains to the agent intellect, as is clear from III *De Anima* [5, 430a 15]. Therefore the agent intellect is God. Now God is one; therefore the agent intellect is one only.

2 Furthermore, nothing which is separated from the body is multiplied in consequence of the multiplication of bodies. But the agent intellect is separated from the body, as is said in III *De Anima* [5, 430a 17]. Therefore the agent intellect is not multiplied in consequence of the multiplication of bodies, and consequently not in consequence of the multiplication of men.

3 Furthermore, there is nothing in our soul which always understands. But this is an attribute of the agent intellect; for it is said in III *De Anima* [5, 430a 22] that "it is not the case that it sometimes understands and sometimes does not." Therefore the agent intellect is not something belonging to the soul, and so is not multiplied in consequence of the multiplication of souls and of men.

4 Furthermore, nothing reduces itself from potency to act. But the possible intellect is reduced to act through the agent intellect, as III *De Anima* [5, 430a 14] makes clear. Therefore the agent intellect is not rooted in the essence of the soul, wherein the possible intellect is rooted; and thus we reach the same conclusion as before.

5 Furthermore, every multiplication follows upon some distinction. But the agent intellect cannot be distinguished through matter, since it is separated; nor through form, for in this case it would be specifically different. Therefore the agent intellect is not multiplied in men.

6 Furthermore, that which is a cause of separation is in the highest degree separated. But the agent intellect is a cause of separation; for it abstracts species from matter. Therefore it is separated, and thus is not multiplied in consequence of the multiplication of men.

---

[1] *In II Sent.*, d. 17, q. 2, a. 1; *De Ver.* X, 6; *Contra Gentiles* II*, cap. 76-78; *Summa Theol.* I, q. 79, 4-5; *Q. De An.* 4, 5*, 16; *In III De An.*, lec. 10; *Compend. Theol.* 86.

Aristotle, *De An. III*, c. 5. Avicenna, *De An.* V, c. 5; *Met.* IX, c. 3. Algazel, II, tr. 5, cc. 1-3. Averroes, *In III De An.*, comm. 17-20, and 36. Guil. Alvernus, *De Universo* II, 1, c. 14 sqq.; *De An.* V, 2 and 7; *ibid.*, VII, 4. Ioan. de Rupella, *De An.* II, c. 37. Alex. Halensis, *Summa* II, 1, p. 451. St. Bonaventure, *In II Sent.*, d. 24, p. 567. Albertus M., *Summa de Creat.* II, q. 55, a. 3, vol. 35, p. 461; *In III De An.*, vol. 5, p. 363; *Summa Theol.* II, tr. 13, q. 77, m. 3, and tr. 15, q. 93, m. 1-2. *Summa Philos.*, tr. 15, c. 11. Roger Bacon, *Opus Maius* II, c. 5; *Opus Tertium*, c. 23.

[2] William of Auvergne and Roger Bacon had made this assertion. Later, many other Augustinians say the same.

7 Furthermore, no power which can act the more, the more it acts, has a limit on its activity. But the agent intellect is of this kind; because "whenever we understand some great intelligible thing, we are not less able to understand, but more", as is said in III *De Anima* [3, 429b 2]. Therefore the agent intellect does not have any limit on its activity. Now actual created being has a limit on its activity, since it is of finite power. Therefore the agent intellect is not something created, and thus is one only.

8 Furthermore, Augustine says in *De Diversis Quaestionibus* LXXXIII [IX, *PL* XL, 13]: "Every thing which the corporeal sense touches . . . is changed without any temporal interruption . . . Now something which is changed without any interruption cannot be comprehended. The clearness of truth is, therefore, not to be expected from the senses of the body." And afterwards he adds: "Nothing is perceptible to the sense, which does not possess a likeness to what is false, with the result that it cannot be distinguished. But nothing can be perceived which is not distinguished from the false. Judgment of the truth, then, is not established in the senses." In this way, therefore, he proves that we cannot judge of truth through sensible things, both because of the fact that they are changeable, and because of the fact that they have something that is similar to falsity. But this holds good of every creature: therefore, through no creature can we judge of truth. But we do judge of truth through the agent intellect: therefore the agent intellect is not something created; and thus we reach the same conclusion as before.

9 Furthermore, Augustine says in IV[3] *De Trinitate* [XIV, 15, 21] that the impious "rightly censure and rightly praise many things in the customs of men. By what standards, pray, do they judge these things, unless by those in which they see how each man should live, even if they themselves do not live in the same way? Where do they see these standards? Not in their own nature, since . . . their minds are evidently changeable, but these rules are unchangeable . . . Nor do they see them in a habit of their mind, since these rules are rules of justice but their minds are evidently unjust . . . Where, therefore, have they been written except in the book of that light which is called truth?" From this it would seem that we are competent to judge of what is just and what is unjust on the basis of a light which is above our minds. Now judgment in speculative as well as in practical matters is an attribute of ours in consequence of the agent intellect. Therefore the agent intellect is a light above our mind. Therefore it is not multiplied along with the multiplication of souls and of' men.

---

[3] It is strange how often in our manuscripts the numeral IV is written for another number.

10 Furthermore, Augustine says in the book *De Vera Religione* [XXXI, XXXII] that, concerning any two things neither of which is the best thing, we cannot judge which of them is better than the other, except through something which is better than both. Now we judge that an angel is better than a soul, although nevertheless neither of them is the best thing. Therefore it must be the case that this judgment is made through something which is better than both, and this is nothing other than God. Since, therefore, we judge through the agent intellect, it would seem that the agent intellect is God; and thus we reach the same conclusion as before.

11 Furthermore, the Philosopher says in III *De Anima* [5, 430a 12] that the agent intellect is to the possible intellect "as art is to the material." But in no kind of artificial production do the art and the material coincide in the same object; nor in general do an agent and material coincide in a numerically same object, as is said in II *Physica* [7, 198a]. Therefore the agent intellect is not something in the essence of the soul in which the possible intellect is; and so it is not multiplied in consequence of the multiplication of souls and of men.

12 Furthermore, Augustine says in III *De Libero Arbitrio* [II, 8, 20, *PL* XXXII, 1251] that "the true essence of number is present to all reasoning persons." But the true essence of number is one. Therefore there must be some one thing whereby it is present to all. Now this is the agent intellect, by the power of which we abstract universal characters from things. Therefore the agent intellect is one in all men.

13 Furthermore, in the same book [IX, 27] it is said: "If the highest good is one thing for all, it must also be the case that the truth wherein it is discerned and comprehended, that is, wisdom, is one truth common to all men." But the highest good is discerned and comprehended by us through the intellect, and especially through the agent intellect. Therefore the agent intellect is one in all men.

14 Furthermore, like naturally tends to cause like. But a universal is one thing in all men. Since, therefore, it is characteristic of the agent intellect to cause a universal, it would seem that the agent intellect is one in all men.

15 Furthermore, if the agent intellect is a part of the soul, it must either be created clothed or filled[4] with species: and in that case it places those species also in the possible intellect, and will not need to abstract intelligible species from the phantasms; or else it is created naked and lacking in species: and in that case it will not be effectually able to abstract species from phantasms, because it will not recognize that species which it is seeking, after it has abstracted it, unless it previously had

---

[4] The text "or filled . . . possible" is not certain, but the sense seems to be entirely clear.

some notion of it; just as a man who is looking for a runaway slave does not recognize him when he has found him, unless previously he had some knowledge of him.[5] Therefore the agent intellect is not a part of the soul; and thus it is not multiplied along with souls and men.

16 Furthermore, once a sufficient cause has been asserted, it is superfluous to assert another cause for the same effect. But there is an extrinsic cause sufficient for the enlightenment of men, namely, God. Therefore it is not necessary to assert that an agent intellect, whose function it is to enlighten, is something in the soul of men; and thus it is not multiplied along with souls and men.

17 Furthermore, if the agent intellect is put down as part of the soul of man, it must be that it contributes to something in the case of man; because nothing among the things created by God is idle and vain. But the agent intellect does not contribute to man's knowing, in the sense that it enlightens the possible intellect: because the possible intellect, once it has been actuated through an intelligible species, is fully able to act on its own account, just as anything else is which has a form. Similarly, it does not make any contribution in the matter of lighting up the phantasms, abstracting intelligible species from them: because, just as a species which is received in a sense imprints its likeness on the imagination, so it would seem that a form which is in the imagination, since it is more spiritual and for this reason more powerful, is able to imprint its likeness on a further power, namely, on the possible intellect. The agent intellect is not, therefore, a part of the soul; and thus it is not multiplied in men.

But on the other hand there is i what the Philosopher says in III De Anima [5, 430a 13],[6] that the agent intellect is a part of the soul. Therefore it is multiplied in consequence of the multiplication of souls.

ii Furthermore, Augustine says in IV De Trinitate [XVI, 21] that "philosophers have not contemplated intellectually, better than others, in those supreme and eternal notions," the things which they have discussed in an historical way;[7] and so it would seem that they have contemplated these things in some light that is connatural to them. Now the light wherein we contemplate truth is the agent intellect. Therefore

---

[5] Compare Avicenna (De An. V, c. 7): "If the soul had not known at some time what it now does not know and seeks to get knowledge of: when it obtained this it would not know that it was the thing which it had sought, as, for example, he who seeks a fugitive prisoner . . ."
[6] Where he asserts: "It is necessary for these differences to be in the soul."
[7] Because empirical and historical knowledge of this sort is distinguished from purely intelligible things, Augustine is saying that the Platonists knew the latter in the eternal ideas, but not the former. And yet, because they knew many things empirically, and this through the aid of an intelligible light, it must be the case that they knew these things by the light of the agent intellect, which is proper and connatural to themselves.

the agent intellect is a part of the soul, and thus we reach the same conclusion as before.

iii Furthermore, Augustine says in XII *De Trinitate* [XV, 24]: "We have to believe that the nature of the intellectual mind is so constituted . . . that it sees the above-mentioned things in a sort of incorporeal light which is unique of its kind, just as the bodily eye sees the things that lie about it in this corporeal light." Now that light whereby our mind understands is the agent intellect. Therefore the agent intellect is something of the nature of the soul,[8] and thus it is multiplied through the multiplication of souls and men.

ANSWER. It must be said that, as has been mentioned before [Art. IX], it is necessary for Aristotle to posit the agent intellect; because he did not assert that the natures of sensible things have a subsistence of their own apart from matter, so as to be actually intelligible, and consequently there had to be some power to make them actually intelligible, by abstracting from individual matter; and this power is called the agent intellect. Some have asserted that this is a sort of separated substance, not multiplied in correspondence with the number of men; but others have asserted that it is in itself a sort of power of the soul, and is multiplied in many men. And both of these assertions are true in a sense.[9]

For it must be the case that above the human soul there is some intellect on which its understanding depends; and this can be made evident on three grounds. First of all, because every thing that belongs to a thing in a partial way is previously in something in a substantial way; thus, for instance, if a piece of iron is fiery hot, there must be something among things which is "fire" in its own nature and substance. Now the human soul is intellectual in a partial way: for it does not understand in every part of itself, but in its highest part only. There must then be something higher than a soul, which is intellect in its whole nature, from which the intellectuality of the soul is derived and upon which its act of understanding depends. Secondly, because it is necessary that prior to everything that is movable there must be something that is immovable in relation to that movement, just as above the things that are subject to alteration there is something not subject

---

[8] According to St. Thomas, the expression "sui generis" signifies "of the genus of the soul itself"; but this seems less probable. For very often Augustine calls even the power of sensing and imagining a kind of "incorporeal light"; but intelligible light is another and far more noble light: "unique of its kind."

[9] In the first paragraph he points out in what sense God is that which enlightens all intellects; and in the second, what must be put in our soul itself. St. Thomas always had the same view about the theory of a separate agent intellect: 1) that the theory is much less absurd than the doctrine of a separated possible intellect; indeed, that it could in a sense be defended; 2) but that it had not been taught by Aristotle; 3) that the agent intellect of which Aristotle speaks cannot be stretched to include this meaning.

to alteration, like a heavenly body; for every movement is caused by something that is immovable. Now the very understanding of the human soul takes place as a movement; for the soul understands by reasoning discursively from effects to causes, and from causes to effects, and from likes to likes, and from opposites to opposites. There must, then, be above the soul some intellect whose power of understanding is fixed and at rest without discursive thinking of this sort. Thirdly, because it is necessary that, although in one and the same being a potency is prior to an act, nevertheless, absolutely speaking, some act is prior to any potency in another being; and similarly, prior to every imperfect thing there must be something that is perfect. Now the human soul at the outset is in potency to intelligible things; and it is found to be imperfect in understanding because never in this life will it attain the truth of all intelligible things. There must be, then, above the soul some intellect that always exists in act and is wholly perfect in its understanding of truth.

However, it cannot be said that that higher intellect makes things actually intelligible in us immediately, apart from some power from it in which our soul has a share. For it is quite generally true even in the case of corporeal things, that in lower things there are to be found particular powers that are active in respect to definite effects, besides the universal active powers; thus, for instance, perfect animals are not generated as a result of the universal power of the sun only, but as a result of the particular power which is in the semen; although some imperfect animals are generated without semen as a result of the power of the sun, and yet even in their generation there is not lacking the action of a particular power that alters and disposes the matter. Now the human soul is the most perfect of those beings which exist among inferior things. Hence it must be the case that in addition to the universal power of the higher intellect, there should be imparted to it some power that is, as it were, particular in respect to this definite effect, namely, that things become actually intelligible. And it is clear from experience[10] that this is true; for one particular man, such as Socrates or Plato, makes things intelligible in act when he pleases, that is, by apprehending[11] a universal form from particulars, when he separates that which is common to all individual men from those things which are peculiar to each. Thus then the action of the agent intellect, which is to abstract the universal, is an action of "this particular man", as is also the act of considering or judging about a common nature, which

---

[10] Compare *Summa Theol.* I, q. 79, a. 4, resp.: "And this we know by experience;" *Q. De An.* 5, resp.: "Now we experience both of these activities in ourselves; for we both receive things that are intelligible and we abstract them."
[11] I believe that for "apprehendo" we should read "abstrahendo."

[116]

is the action of the possible intellect. Now every agent that does any action has within itself by way of a form the power which is the principle of this kind of action. Hence, just as it is necessary that the possible intellect be something that is formally inherent in man, as we showed above, so it is necessary that the agent intellect be something that is formally inherent in man. A connection by way of phantasms does not suffice for this, as Averroes imagines, as was also shown above in regard to the possible intellect [Art. II and IX]. And it seems clear that Aristotle realized this when he said [III *De An.*, 5, 430a 13] that "there must be these differences in the soul," namely, the agent and the possible intellects; and again he says [430a 15] that the agent intellect is "as it were, a brightness which is a participated light." But Plato, as Themistius says in his *Commentum de Anima* [III, 5], considering the intellect apart and not considering the participated power of the soul, compared the intellect to the sun.

But we must consider what that separated intellect is, upon which the human soul's understanding depends. For some have said that this intellect is the lowest of the separated substances,[12] which is connected with our souls by its own light. But this is contrary to the truth of faith in many respects. First of all because, since this intellectual light pertains to the nature of the soul, it comes from Him alone by Whom the nature of the soul is created. Now God alone is the creator of the soul, and not some separated substance which we call an angel; hence it is said significantly in *Genesis* I [II, 7] that God Himself "breathed into the face of man the breath of life." Hence the only remaining alternative is that the light of the agent intellect is not caused in the soul by any other separated substance, but is caused immediately by God. Secondly, because the ultimate perfection of each individual agent is that it can attain to its own principle. Now the ultimate perfection or beatitude of man is based on intellectual activity, as the Philosopher also says in *Ethica* X [7]. If, then, the principle and cause of the intellectuality of men were some other separated substance, it would have to be the case that the ultimate beatitude of man would be situated in that created substance; and those who hold this view clearly assert this: for they assert that the ultimate felicity of man is to be connected with the agent intelligence.[13] Now the true faith asserts that the ultimate

---

[12] Namely, the tenth intelligence, "which is related to our souls and to the whole sphere of active and passive things as the higher separated substances, which they call intelligences, are related to the souls of the heavenly bodies which they assert as animate, and to the heavenly bodies themselves." *Q. De An.* 5, resp. He refers especially to the doctrine of Avicenna.

[13] In this all the Arabian Peripatetics agree. Cf. Avicenna (*De An.* V, c. 6): "Now when the soul will be freed from the body and from the accidents of the body, then it will be able to be conjoined to the agent intelligence; and then it will find therein intelligible beauty and perennial delight."

[117]

beatitude of man is in God alone, according to this quotation from *John* XVII [3]: "This is the eternal life, that they may know Thee, the only true God"; and that in participating in this beatitude, men are "equal to the angels," as is held by *Luke* XX [36]. Thirdly, because if man were to have a share in the intellectual light from an angel, it would follow that man as regards his mind would not be made to the image of God Himself, but to the image of angels, contrary to what is said in *Genesis* I [26]: "Let us make man to our image and likeness," that is, to the common image of the Trinity, not to the image of the angels.

And hence we say that the light of the agent intellect, of which Aristotle is speaking, is impressed upon us immediately by God, and by this light we discern truth from falsity, and good from evil. And concerning this it is said in the *Psalms* [IV, 6, 7]: "Many say, Who showeth us good things? The light of Thy countenance, O Lord, is signed upon us," i.e., by which good things are shown to us. Thus, then, that which makes things actually intelligible in us after the manner of a participated light is a part of the soul, and is multiplied along with the number of souls and of men. But that which makes things intelligible after the manner of the sun, which illuminates, is something that is one and separate, which is God. Hence Augustine says in I *Soliloquia* [VI, 12]: "Reason promises . . . to show God to my mind as the sun is shown to the eyes; for the eyes of the mind, so to speak, are the senses of the soul. But all the most certain branches of learning are of such a nature as things illumined by the sun, so that they can be seen . . . and God Himself is the one who illumines." Now this one separate principle of our knowledge cannot be understood to be the agent intellect of which the Philosopher is speaking, as Themistius says [*In De An.* III, 5], because God is not in the nature of the soul; but the agent intellect is the name given by Aristotle to the light that is received in our soul from God. And in view of this it remains to be said without qualification that the agent intellect is not one in all men.

As to the first argument, therefore, it must be said that it is proper to God to enlighten men by impressing on them the natural light of the agent intellect, and in addition to this the light of grace and glory. But the agent intellect lights up the phantasms, as a light that is impressed by God.

As to the second, it must be said that the agent intellect is called "separated" by Aristotle,[14] not as though it were a kind of substance that has actual being outside the body, but because it is not an act of

---

[14] This famous passage is explained more fully in *Contra Gentiles* II, cap. 78. The principal difficulty in the interpretation given is that according to it Aristotle would be distinguishing in that brief paragraph not two intellects only, namely, the possible and the agent, but four: the possible intellect, the agent intellect, the intellect in act, the passive intellect.

any part of the body in the sense that its activity takes place through some corporeal organ, as was said of the possible intellect.

As to the third, it must be said that Aristotle does not make that statement about the agent intellect, but about the intellect in act. For first he spoke of the possible intellect, and afterwards of the agent intellect, and finally he begins to speak of the intellect in act, when he says [III *De An.*, 5, 430a 20]: "Actual knowledge of a thing is identical with its object." And he distinguishes the intellect in act from the intellect in potency in three ways. First of all, because the intellect in potency is not the thing that is understood in potency, but the intellect in act, or knowledge in act, is the thing that is understood or known in act. So too he had said of the senses that the sense in potency and the thing that can be sensed in potency are different. Secondly, he compares the intellect in act to the intellect in potency, because the intellect in potency is temporally prior in one and the same man to the intellect in act; for temporally an intellect is in potency before it is in act. But naturally act is prior to potency; and speaking in an absolute sense, we must posit some intellect in act prior even in time to an intellect in potency, which is reduced to act through some intellect in act. And this is what he adds [430a 21]: "And this in potency is temporally prior in one individual; but in general it is not prior even temporally." And he employs this comparison between potency and act also in IX *Metaphysica* [8, 1049b] and in many other places. Thirdly, he points out a difference in this respect, that the intellect in potency or the possible intellect is sometimes to be found understanding and sometimes not; but this cannot be said of the intellect in act. Just as the visual power sometimes sees and sometimes does not see; but the sight in act consists in actually seeing. And this is what he says [430a 22]: "But it is not true that it sometimes understands and sometimes does not;" and afterwards he adds: "But that thing only is separate which truly is;" and this cannot be understood either of the agent intellect or of the possible intellect, since above he has called both separate; but it must be understood of every thing which is required for the intellect in act, that is, of the whole intellectual part. And hence also he adds [430a 23]: "And this alone is immortal and eternal;" and if this be explained as referring to the agent intellect, it will follow that the possible intellect is corruptible, as Alexander understood; but this is contrary to what Aristotle had said above about the possible intellect. Now it has been necessary to explain these words of Aristotle here in order that they may not be an occasion of error to anyone.

As to the fourth, it must be said that nothing prevents any two things that are related to each other from being such that each of them is both a potency and an act as regards the other, on different grounds;

[119]

thus fire, for instance, is potentially cold and actually hot, but water the opposite; and for this reason natural agents are at the same time passive and active. If, then, the intellectual part be compared to the phantasms, in one respect it will be in potency and in another it will be in act with reference to them. A phantasm actually contains a likeness of a definite nature; but this likeness of a definite species is in the phantasm in potency, able to be abstracted from material conditions. But on the intellectual side the opposite is the case; for it does not actually possess likenesses of distinct things; but yet it actually possesses an immaterial light which has the power of abstracting those things which are able to be abstracted in potency.[15] And thus nothing prevents there being found in the same essence of the soul a possible intellect, which is in potency with respect to the species which are abstracted from the phantasms, and an agent intellect, which abstracts the species from the phantasms. We should have something similar if there were one and the same body which would be transparent, being in potency to all colors; and if along with this it would have a light whereby it could illuminate colors, as is somehow apparent in the eye of a cat.[16]

As to the fifth, it must be said that the light of the agent intellect is multiplied immediately through the multiplication of the souls, which participate in the very light of the agent intellect. Now souls are multiplied along with bodies, as was said above.

As to the sixth, it must be said that this very fact that the light of the agent intellect is not an act of any corporeal organ through which it acts is sufficient for its being able to separate intelligible species from phantasms; since the separateness of intelligible species, which are received in the possible intellect, is not greater than the separateness of the agent intellect.

As to the seventh, it must be said that that argument would be more conclusive as regards the possible intellect than the agent intellect. For the Philosopher brings in this point concerning the possible intellect, that when it has understood the most intelligible thing it will not less understand the least intelligible thing. But no matter what this refers to, it does not follow that the power of the intellect by means of which we understand is infinite in an absolute sense, but that it is infinite with reference to some genus. For nothing prevents a power, which is in itself finite, from not having a limit in some definite genus, but never-

---

[15] Compare *Summa Theol.* I, q. 79, a. 4, ad 4: "The intellectual soul is indeed actually immaterial, but it is in potency with respect to definite species of things; the phantasms, however, on the other hand, are actually likenesses of certain species, but are potentially immaterial."

[16] Compare *Q. De An.* 5: "And something like this is apparent, in a sense, in the case of animals that see by night. Their pupils are in potency with respect to all colors, insofar as they have no definite color in act; but through a kind of light that is in them they somehow make colors actually visible."

theless it does have a limit inasmuch as it cannot extend itself to a higher genus: thus sight does not have a limit in the genus "color" because, if colors were multiplied to infinity, they could all be known by the sight; but yet the sight cannot know those things which belong to a higher genus, as, for instance, the universals. Similarly our intellect does not have a limit in respect to the intelligible things which are connatural to itself, which are abstracted from things that can be sensed; but nevertheless it has a limit, because, in regard to higher intelligible things, which are separated substances, it fails; for it is related to the most manifest of things "as the eye of the owl to the light of the sun", as is said in II *Metaphysica* [1, 993b 9].

As to the eighth, it must be said that that argument is not to the point. For to pass judgment on a truth "by means of" something is used in two senses. In one sense, as "through the medium of"; thus we pass judgment on conclusions "by means of" principles, and on things that are regulated "by means of" a rule. And this seems to be the sense in which Augustine's arguments are carried on. For that which is changeable or that which has a likeness to the false cannot be an infallible rule of truth. But in another sense, to pass judgment on some truth "by means of something" is used thus: "by means of our power of judging," and in this sense we pass judgment on a truth by means of the agent intellect.

But yet in order to examine more searchingly the meaning of Augustine and what the truth is on this point, it must be noted that certain ancient philosophers, who did not assert any way of knowing except sensation nor any entities besides sensible things, declared that no certainty concerning truth could be had by us; and this for two reasons. First of all, because they asserted that sensible things are always in flux and that there is nothing stable in things. Secondly, because some people are to be found who make different judgments about the same thing; thus, for instance, someone who is awake judges in one way and one who is asleep in another, and one who is sick judges in one way and he who is well in another. Nor can anything be had to determine which of them has the truer estimate, since every one of them has some appearance of truth. And these are the the two reasons which Augustine touches on, because of which the ancients said that truth cannot be known by us. And hence too, Socrates, despairing of grasping the truth of things, devoted himself entirely to moral philosophy. But Plato, his disciple, agreeing with the ancient philosophers that sensible things are always in flux and that the sense power has no certain judgment of things, in order to establish the certainty of scientific knowledge posited on the one hand species of things separated from sensible things and immovable, and he said that the sciences are about these; on the other

[121]

hand he posited in man a knowing power higher than sense, namely, the mind or intellect, illumined by a kind of higher intelligible sun, as the sight is illumined by the visible sun.

Augustine, however, following Plato as far as the Catholic Faith allowed, did not posit species of things with a subsistence of their own, but instead of them he posited ideas of things in the divine mind and said that through these, by an intellect that is illumined by divine light, we form judgments about all things; not indeed in such a way that we see the ideas themselves, for this would be impossible unless we were to see the essence of God, but according to what these supreme ideas imprint upon our minds. For Plato held that the sciences were concerned with the separate species in this sense: not that these latter could be seen themselves; but according as our mind participates in them it has knowledge of things. And hence too in a certain gloss on this passage: "Truths are lessened by the sons of men" [August., *Enarr. in Psalm* XI, 1], it is said that just as from one face many likenesses shine forth in mirrors, so from the one primary truth there result many truths in our minds. Aristotle, however, proceeded along another way.[17] For first he showed in many ways that there is something stable in sensible things. Secondly, that the judgment of the sense is true concerning proper objects of sense, but that it is mistaken about common objects of sense, and more so about things that can be sensed by accident. Thirdly, that above the sense there is an intellectual power which makes judgments concerning truth, not through any intelligible things that exist outside, but through the light of the agent intellect, which makes things intelligible. Now it does not matter much if we say that intelligible things themselves are participated in from God, or that the light which makes them intelligible is participated in from God.[18]

As to the ninth, it must be said that those rules which the impious see are the first principles of action, and that they are seen through the light of the agent intellect that is participated from God, just as are also the first principles of the speculative sciences.

As to the tenth, it must be said that that whereby one judges which of two things is the better ought to be better than both, if one judges

---

[17] And from this explanation it is obvious that St. Thomas clearly perceived the profound differences between his own Peripateticism and St. Augustine's doctrine of knowledge, although he usually interprets the sayings of Augustine on divine light and illumination according to his own principles. The same is clear from *De Ver.* (X, 6, resp.), which refers especially to the Augustinian doctrine: "But others have said that the soul is unto itself a cause of knowledge *(scientia)*. For it does not receive knowledge from sensible things, as though by the action of sense objects the likenesses of things somehow reach the soul; but the soul itself in the presence of sense objects forms" and so on.

[18] Evidently the difference will depend upon the meaning which is assigned to such formulas.

by this as by a rule or a measure. For in this sense white is the rule or measure of all other colors, and God of all beings; because each individual thing is better, the nearer it approaches the best thing. But that whereby we judge a given thing to be better than another, as by a knowing power, need not be better than both. Now in this way we judge through the agent intellect that an angel is better than a soul.

As to the eleventh, the solution is clear from what has been said: for the agent intellect is related to the possible intellect as an agent and a mover is related to the material, inasmuch as it makes intelligible in act things to which the possible intellect is in potency. Now it has been said how these two can be rooted in the one substance of the soul.

As to the twelfth, it must be said that there is one essence of numbers in all minds, just as there is also one essence of a stone; and this essence is one on the part of the thing that is understood, but not on the part of the act of understanding, which is not essential to the thing that is understood; for it is not essential to a stone that it be understood.[19] And hence this sort of unity of the essence of numbers or of stones or of anything whatever does not make for a unity of the possible or of the agent intellect, as was explained more fully above [Art. IX, ad 6].

As to the thirteenth, it must be said that that truth wherein the highest good is apprehended is common to all minds, either by reason of the oneness of the thing or by reason of the oneness of the primary light which flows into all minds.

As to the fourteenth, it must be said that the universal, which the agent intellect causes, is one thing in all the beings from which it is abstracted; and hence the agent intellect is not diversified on the basis of their diversification. However, it is diversified on the basis of a diversity of intellects: because even the universal does not derive its oneness from the standpoint of its being understood by me and by you; for it is accidental to the universal that it is understood by me and by you. And hence the diversity of intellects does not affect the oneness of the universal.

As to the fifteenth, it must be said that it is incorrect to say that the agent intellect is naked or clothed, full of species or empty of them.[20] For to be filled with species is characteristic of the possible intellect, but to cause them is characteristic of the agent intellect. Now it must not be said that the agent intellect understands in isolation from the

---

[19] Yet St. Augustine carefully distinguishes between the knowledge of purely intelligible things (numbers), and of empirical things (stones), a distinction which loses its importance in the Peripatetic teaching.
[20] He is perhaps thinking of prop. 9 of the *Liber de Causis*, "every intelligence is full of forms" and the statement made by Aristotle that the intellect is the "place of species".

possible intellect. but that the man understands by means of both; it is he who has knowledge in particular, through the sense powers, of those things which are abstracted by means of the agent intellect.

As to the sixteenth, it must be said that it is not because of God's insufficiency that He attributes powers of action to created things, but because of His most perfect fullness, which is sufficient for sharing with all beings.

As to the seventeenth, it must be said that a species which is in the imagination is of the same genus as a species which is in a sense, because both are individual and material. But a species which is in an intellect belongs to another genus, because it is universal. And consequently an imagined species cannot imprint an intelligible species as a sensitive species imprints an imagined species; and for this reason an active intellectual power is necessary, whereas an active sense power is not.

ARTICLE XI

THE last question is: Are the powers of the soul the same as the essence of the soul?[1] No

And it would seem that they are. *1* For Augustine says in IX *De Trinitate* [IV, 5]: "We are reminded . . . that these things (namely, mind, knowledge, and love) exist in the soul . . . substantially or essentially, not as in a subject, like color or shape in a body or like any other quantity or quality."

2 Furthermore, in the book *De Spiritu et Anima* [XIII, PL XL, 789] it is said that "God is all the things that He has, but the soul is some of the things that it has",[2] namely, powers; and is not some of the things that it has, namely, virtues.

3 Futhermore, substantial differences are not derived from any accidents. But "sensible" and "rational" are substantial differences, and they are derived from sense and reason. Therefore sense and reason are not accidents, and by a parallel argument, neither are the other powers of the soul; and so they seem to belong to the essence of the soul.

But the objector said that the powers of the soul are not accidents and do not belong to the essence of the soul, but that they are natural or substantial properties;[3] and so they are something intermediate between a subject and an accident. But on the other hand, *4* between an affirmation and a denial there is nothing intermediate. But a substance and an accident are differentiated by way of affirmation and denial: because an accident is that which is in a subject, but a substance is that which is not in a subject. Therefore between the essence of a thing and an accident there is nothing intermediate.

5 Furthermore, if the powers of the soul are called natural or essential properties, this is either because they are essential parts, or because they are caused by the principles of the essence. If in the first sense, then they pertain to the essence of the soul, because essential parts are of the essence of a thing. If in the second sense, then even accidents can be called essential, because they are caused by the prin-

---

[1] *In I Sent.*, d. 3, q. 4, a. 2; *Quodl.* VII, a. 5; *Quodl.* X, a. 5; *Summa Theol.* I, q. 77, a. 1*, q. 79, a. 1 (and on the angels, q. 54, a. 3); *Q. De An.* 12*.
    St. Augustine, *De Trin.* IX, iv; X, xi, 18, etc. Avicenna, *De An.* V, c. 7. Peter Lombard, *Sent.* I, d. 3. Isaac de Stella, *Epist. De An., PL* 194, 1883. Alcherus de Claravalle, *De Spiritu et Anima* 13. Phil. Cancellarius, q. 3 and q. 4 *De An.* Guil. Alvernus, *De An.* III, c. 6. Ioan. de Rupella, *De An.* II, c. 1. Alex. Halensis, *Summa* II, 1, p. 424. Albertus M., *Summa de Creat.* II, q. 7, vol. 35, p. 89; *In I De An.*, tr. 3, cc. 15-16. St. Bonaventure, *In I Sent.*, d. 3, p. 84; *In II Sent.*, d. 24, p. 558 (and compare the scholia at that place in the Quaracchi edition). *Summa Philos.* VI, c. 6. Roger Bacon, *Com. Nat.* IV, 3, c. 5.
[2] In that passage Alcher emphatically asserts that the powers are identical with the essence.
[3] Thus Lombard (*Sent.* I, d. 3); they are "natural properties or powers."

ciples of a subject. Therefore it must be the case that the powers of the soul either pertain to the essence of the soul, or else are accidents.

But the objector said that, although accidents are caused by the principles of a substance, yet not every thing which is caused by the principles of a substance is an accident. But on the other hand, 6 every thing that is intermediate must be distinguished from both extremes. If, then, the powers of the soul are intermediate between an essence and an accident, it must be the case that they are differentiated from an essence as well as from an accident. But nothing can be differentiated from a thing by something that is common to both. Since, then, to flow from the principles of a substance, which is the reason why the powers are said to be essential, is an attribute even of accidents, it would seem that the powers of the soul are not differentiated from accidents; and so it would seem that there is no intermediate between substance and accident.

But the objector said that they are differentiated from accidents by the fact that a soul can be conceived apart from accidents, but cannot be conceived apart from its own powers. But on the other hand, 7 each individual thing is understood through its own essence, because the proper object of the intellect is what a thing is, as is said in III *De Anima* [4, 429b 19]. Whatever there is, then, apart from which a thing cannot be understood, belongs to the essence of that thing.

If, then, the soul cannot be understood apart from its powers, it follows that the powers belong to the essence of the soul and that they are not something intermediate between essence and accidents.

8 Furthermore, Augustine says in X *De Trinitate* [XI, 18] that memory, understanding, and will are "one life, one mind, one substance." And so it would seem that the powers of the soul are its very essence.

9 Furthermore, as the whole soul is to the whole body, so a part of the soul is to a part of the body. But the whole soul is the substantial form of the body. Therefore a part of the soul, e.g., sight, is the substantial form of a part of the body, namely, of the eye. But the soul by its own essence is the substantial form of the whole body and of every one of its parts. Therefore the power of sight is identical with the essence of the soul; and for the same reason so are all the other powers.

10 Furthermore, the soul is nobler than an accidental form. But an active accidental form is its own power of action. Therefore, so much the more is the soul its own powers.

11 Furthermore, Anselm says in his *Monologium* [LXVII, *PL* CLVIII, 213] that nothing greater could be given to the soul than remembering, understanding, and willing. But among all the things that

[126]

belong to the soul, the chief thing is its own essence, which has been given to it by God. Therefore the powers of the soul are identical with its essence.

12 Furthermore, if the powers of the soul are something other than its essence, it must be the case that they flow from the essence of the soul as from a principle. But this is impossible, because it would follow that a principiate would be more immaterial than its own principle: for the intellect, which is one of the powers, is not an act of any body; whereas the soul by its own essence is the act of the body. Therefore, too, the first statement is incongruous, namely, that the powers of the soul are not its essence.

13 Furthermore, it is especially proper to a substance to be something that is able to take on contraries. But the powers of the soul are able to take on contraries: thus the will, for instance, is able to take on virtue and vice, and the intellect, knowledge and error. Therefore, the powers of the soul are a substance. But they are not a different substance from the substance of the soul. Therefore they are identical with the very substance of the soul.

14 Furthermore, the soul is united to the body as its form immediately, and not through the medium of some power. Now inasmuch as it is the form of the body, it gives some act to the body. But not the act of existence, because this act is found even in things that have no soul; and again, it does not give the act of being alive, because this act is found in things wherein there is no rational soul. Therefore, the only remaining alternative is that it gives the act of understanding. But this act is given by the intellectual power. Therefore the intellectual power is identical with the essence of the soul.

15 Furthermore, the soul is nobler and more perfect than prime matter. But prime matter is identical with its own potency. For it cannot be said that the potency of matter is an accident of it, because in that case an accident would exist prior to a substantial form, since potency in one and the same thing is temporally prior to act, as is said in IX *Metaphysica* [8, 1049b 19]; and in the second place, neither is it the substantial form, because a form is an act, which is the opposite of a potency; and similarly neither is it a composite substance, because in that case a composite substance would precede a form, which is impossible. And thus the only remaining alternative is that the potency of matter is the very essence of matter. Much more, then, are the powers of the soul its essence.

16 Furthermore, an accident does not extend beyond its own subject.[4] But the powers of the soul extend beyond the soul itself, be-

---

[4] He is talking about the famous passage of St. Augustine (*De Trin.* IX, iv, 5): "For whatever there is of this kind (quantity or quality) does not exceed the subject in which it is. For that particular color or the shape of this particular

[127]

cause the soul not only understands and wills itself, but also other things. Therefore the powers of the soul are not its accidents. The only remaining alternative, therefore, is that they are the very essence of the soul.

17 Furthermore, every substance is intellectual by the very fact that it is free from matter, as Avicenna says [VIII *Met.*, 6]. But immaterial actual being is proper to the soul by its own essence: therefore, intellectual actual being is also proper to it. Therefore the intellect is its own essence, and by a parallel argument so are its other powers.

18 Furthermore, "in those things which are without matter, the intellect and the thing that is understood are the same thing," according to the Philosopher [III *De An.*, 4, 430a 2]. But the very essence of the soul is what is understood. Therefore the very essence of the soul is the understanding intellect; and by a parallel argument the soul is its other powers.

19 Furthermore, the parts of a thing belong to its substance. But the powers of the soul are said to be its parts. Therefore they pertain to the substance of the soul.

20 Furthermore, the soul is a simple substance, as was said above; but the powers of the soul are several. If, then, the powers of the soul are not its essence, but are kinds of accidents, it follows that in one simple thing there are several and different accidents, which seems incongruous. Therefore the powers of the soul are not its accidents but its very essence.

But on the other hand there is *i* what Dionysius says in the eleventh chapter of *De Caelesti Hierarchia* [§2, *PG* I, 283D], that the higher essences are divided into substance, power, and activity. Much more, then, in souls, their essence is one thing and the virtue or power is another.

ii Furthermore, Augustine says in XV *De Trinitate* [XXIII, 43] that the soul is called the image of God, as a board is, "because of the picture which is on it." But a picture is not the very essence of the board. Therefore neither are the powers of the soul, by which the image of God is stamped upon the soul, the soul's very substance.[5]

---

body cannot belong to another body also. But the mind through the love with which it loves itself can also love something other than itself. Likewise the mind not only knows itself, but many other things also. Wherefore, love and knowledge are not in the mind as in a subject, but also exist substantially, as the mind itself does because, although they are used in relation to each other, yet each is individually in its own substance."

[5] Both in Augustine and in the Lombard the question is raised not on its own account, but in relation to determining the image of the Holy Trinity in the soul; and they did not want to admit that that image is merely in the accidents of the soul. This St. Thomas clearly intimates in *Q. De An.* 10, obj. 6. St. Bonaventure *In II Sent.*, d. 24, p. 559) begins his answer thus: "It must be said that, although the aforesaid question has more of curiosity than of usefulness in it on account

iii Furthermore, all things that are counted like essences are not one essence. But the three things in view of which the image is considered to be in the soul are counted like essences or substances. Therefore they are not the very essence of the soul, which is one.

iv Furthermore, a power is something intermediate between a substance and an activity. But an activity differs from the substance of the soul. Therefore a power differs from both; otherwise it would not be something intermediate if it were identical with an extreme.

v Furthermore, a principal and an instrumental agent are not one thing. But a power of the soul is related to its essence as an instrumental agent is to a principal agent; for Anselm says in his book *De Concordia Praescientiae et Liberi Arbitrii* [XI, *PL* 158, 534] that the will, which is a power of the soul, is like an instrument. Therefore the soul is not its own powers.

vi Furthermore, the Philosopher says in the first chapter of *De Memoria et Reminiscentia* [*in fin.*] that memory is a passion or a habit of the sense faculty or of the imaginative faculty. Now a passion and a habit is an accident. Therefore memory is an accident; and for the same reason so are the other powers of the soul.

ANSWER. It must be said that some have asserted that the powers of the soul are nothing else than its very essence: in such a way that one and the same essence of the soul, according as it is the principle of sense activity, is called the sense; but according as it is the principle of the intellectual activity, it is called intellect; and so of the other faculties.[6] And they seem to have been especially moved toward this position, as Avicenna says [*De An.* V, 7], because of the simplicity of the soul, as though this simplicity would not permit such great diversity as is apparent in the powers of the soul. But this position is utterly impossible.

First of all, because it is impossible in the case of any created substance that its own essence should be its own active power. For it is obvious that different acts belong to different things; for an act is always proportioned to the thing whereof it is an act. Now just as actual being itself is a kind of actuality of an essence, so acting is an actuality of an active power or virtue. For on this basis both of these are in act: the essence in regard to actual being, and the power in regard to acting. And hence, since in no creature is its own activity its own actual being, but this is proper to God alone, it follows that the active power of no creature is its essence; but to God alone is it proper that His essence is His power.

---

of the fact that whether one side or the other is taken, no prejudice either to faith or morals arises" etc.

[6] So says William of Auvergne (*De An.* III, 6), who vehemently attacks a real distinction. Avicenna teaches that the powers are really distinct from the essence.

maintain diversity what soul does (powers)

Secondly, this appears impossible for a special reason in the case of the soul, on three counts. ①First of all, because an essence is one; whereas in regard to powers we must assert manyness because of the diversity of acts and objects. For powers must be diversified on the basis of their acts, since a potency is so called in relation to an act. ②Secondly, the same thing is apparent as a result of the diversity of powers, whereof certain ones are acts of certain parts of the body,[7] as are all powers of the sensitive and the nutritive part; but certain powers are not acts of any part of the body, as, for instance, the intellect and the will. This could not be the case if the powers of the soul were nothing less than its essence; for it cannot be said that one and the same thing may be an act of the body and yet something separate, except in different respects.

③ Thirdly, the same is apparent as a result of the order of the powers of the soul and their relation to one another. For it is found that one power moves another: thus, for instance, reason moves the irascible and the concupiscible power, and the intellect moves the will; and this could not be the case if all the powers were the very essence of the soul, because the same thing does not move itself in the same respect, as the Philosopher proves [VIII *Phys.*, 5]. Therefore the only remaining alternative is that the powers of the soul are not its very essence.

Some, granting this, say that they are not an accident of the soul either, but are its essential or natural properties.[8] This opinion, in fact, if understood in one sense, can be maintained, but in another sense it is impossible. As evidence of this we must bear in mind that "accident" is taken in two senses by philosophers. In one sense, as that which is the opposite of "substance" and includes under itself nine categories of things. Now taking "accident" in this sense the position is impossible. For between a substance and an accident there cannot be anything intermediate, since substance and accident are divisions of being by way of affirmation and denial: since it is proper to a substance not to be in a subject, but to an accident to be in a subject. And hence, if the powers of the soul are not the very essence of the soul (and it is obvious that they are not other substances), it follows that they are accidents included under one of the nine categories.[9] For they are in the second species of quality, which is called natural power or natural impotence. "Accident" is taken in another sense as being one of the four predicates put down by Aristotle in I *Topica* [4, 101b 17], and as being one of the five

---

[7] Cf. Aristotle (II *De An.*, c. 1, 413a 5-7): "For some parts have an act of their own. But as regards some parts, there is nothing to prevent (the soul from being separated), because of the fact that they are not acts of any part of the body."
[8] Cf. Peter Lombard (I *Sent.*, d. 3).
[9] This is called by Roger Bacon (*Comm. Nat.* IV, 3, c. 5): "the damnable view that is popularly accepted at Paris."

[130]

universals put down by Porphyry [*Isagoge,* IV]. For in this sense an accident does not signify that which is common to the nine categories, but the accidental relationship of a predicate to a subject, or the relationship of a universal to those things which are included under the universal. For if this meaning of accident were the same as the first, since accident in this sense is opposed to genus and species, it would follow that nothing which is in the nine categories could be called either a genus or a species; and it is clear that this is false, since color is the genus of whiteness, and number the genus of "couple". Taking accident in this sense, then, there is something intermediate between substance and accident, that is, between a substantial predicate and an accidental predicate; and this is a property. A property is like a substantial predicate, inasmuch as it is caused by the essential principles of a species; and consequently a property is demonstrated as belonging to a subject through a definition that signifies the essence. But it is like an accidental predicate in this sense, that it is neither the essence of a thing, nor a part of the essence, but something outside of the essence itself. Whereas it differs from an accidental predicate, because an accidental predicate is not caused by the essential principles of a species, but it accrues to an individual thing as a property accrues to a species, yet sometimes separably, and sometimes inseparably. So, then, the powers of the soul are intermediate between the essence of the soul and an accident, as natural or essential properties, that is, as properties that are a natural consequence of the essence of the soul.

· As to the first argument, therefore, it must be said that no matter what be said of the powers of the soul, still no one ever thinks (unless he is crazy) that a habit and an act of the soul are its very essence. Now it is obvious that the knowledge and love of which Augustine speaks in that passage do not designate powers, but acts or habits. And hence Augustine does not mean to say that knowledge and love are the very essence of the soul, but that they are in it, and substantially or essentially. To understand this, we must notice that Augustine in that passage is speaking of the mind according as it knows and loves itself. From this viewpoint, then, knowledge and love can be related to the mind, either as to the mind that loves and knows, or as to the mind that is loved and known. And Augustine is speaking here in this second sense; for the reason why he says that knowledge and love exist substantially or essentially in the mind or in the soul is that the mind loves its essence, or knows its substance.[10] And hence he later adds [*De Trin.*

---

[10] In this famous passage there was either a lacuna or some corrupted word in the first copy. The same interpretation is put on Augustine in *Sum. Theol.* I. q. 77, a. 1, ad 1: "It must be said that Augustine is speaking of the mind according as it knows itself and loves itself. Thus therefore knowledge and love, inasmuch as they are referred to the mind itself as that which is known and loved, are sub-

[131]

IX, 4, 7]: "How those three things are not of the same essence I do not see, since the mind loves itself, and itself knows itself."

As to the second, it must be said that the book *De Spiritu et Anima* is apocryphal,[11] since its author is unknown; and there are in it many things falsely or inaccurately stated, because he who wrote the book did not understand the sayings of the saints from whom he tried to quote. Yet if the objection has to be met, we must note that there are three kinds of wholes. One is a universal whole, which is present to every part in its whole essence and power; hence it is properly predicated of its parts, as when one says: Man is an animal. But another whole is an integral whole, which is not present to any part of itself, either in its whole essence or its whole power; and consequently there is no way in which it is predicated of a part. as if one were to say: A wall is a house. The third whole is a potential whole, which is intermediate between these two: for it is present to a part of itself in its whole essence, but not in its whole power. And hence it stands in an intermediate position as a predicate: for it is sometimes predicated of its parts, but not properly, and in this sense it is sometimes said that the soul is its own powers, or vice versa.

As to the third, it must be said that because substantial forms in themselves are unknown but become known to us by their proper accidents, substantial differences are frequently taken from accidents instead of from the substantial forms which become known through such accidents; as, for example, "biped" and "able to walk" and the like; and so also "sensible" and "rational" are put down as substantial differences. Or it may be said that "sensible" and "rational", insofar as they are differences, are not derived from reason and sense according as these are names of powers, but from the rational soul and from the sentient soul.

As to the fourth, it must be said that that argument is based on "accident" in the sense of what is common to the nine categories; and in this sense there is nothing intermediate between substance and accident; but in another sense, as has been said, there is.

As to the fifth, it must be said that the powers of the soul can be called essential properties, not because they are essential parts, but because they are caused by the essence; and in this respect they are not differentiated from "accident" that is common to the nine categories; but they are differentiated from "accident" that is an accidental predicate which is not caused by the specific nature.

---

stantially or essentially in the soul; because the very substance or essence of the soul is known and loved." And yet in that passage another interpretation is added. And in *Q. De An.* (12. ad 5) the above exposition is prefaced by this formula: "And hence perhaps it is in this sense that he said . .."

[11] Cf. above, Art. 3, ad 6.

And hence the solution to the sixth is clear.

As to the seventh, it must be said that there are two activities of the intellect,[12] as is said in III *De Anima* [6, 430a 26]. One whereby it understands what a thing is: and by this sort of activity of the intellect the essence of a thing can be known, both apart from a property and apart from an accident, since neither of these enters into the essence of a thing; and this is the sense on which the argument is based. The other is an activity of the intellect that combines and separates; and in this way a substance can be understood apart from an accidental predicate, even if it is really inseparable: thus, "a crow is white" is intelligible; for there is no repugnance of concepts there, since the opposite of the predicate does not depend on the principles of the species which is designated by the word put down as the subject. But by this activity of the intellect a substance cannot be understood without its property; for it cannot be understood that "man has not the power of laughing", or that "a triangle does not have three angles equal to two right angles"; for here there is repugnance of concepts, because the opposite of the predicate depends upon the nature of the subject. So, then, by the first sort of activity of the intellect the essence of the soul can be understood, in such a way, that is, that its essence is understood apart from its powers; but not by the second kind of activity, i.e., so that it is understood not to have powers.

As to the eighth, it must be said that those three things are said to be one life, one essence, either on the ground that they are related to the essence as to an object, or in the way in which a potential whole is predicated of its parts.

As to the ninth, it must be said that the whole soul is the substantial form of the whole body, not by reason of the totality of its powers, but by the very essence of the soul, as was said above [Art. IV]. And hence it does not follow that the power of sight itself is the substantial form of the eye, but that the very essence of the soul is, according as it is the subject or principle of this power.

As to the tenth, it must be said that an accidental form, which is a principle of action, is itself a power or a virtue of an active substance; but there is no going on to infinity, as though for every virtue there were another virtue.[13]

As to the eleventh, it must be said that an essence is in a sense a greater gift than a power, just as a cause is more important than an

---

[12] Cf. above, Art. 9, resp.
[13] Here he touches on a difficulty that afterwards became classical: if the same soul cannot act on many different things save through the medium of different powers, for the same reason it will not be able to put forth many powers from itself save through the medium of other powers, and so on to infinity.

[133]

effect. But powers are more important, in a sense, inasmuch as they are nearer to the acts whereby the soul holds fast to its end.

As to the twelfth, it must be said that the reason why it happens that a power which is not an act of the body flows from the essence of the soul is that the essence of the soul transcends the limitations of the body, as was said above [Art. II; Art. IX, ad 15]. And hence it does not follow that a power is more immaterial than the essence; but from the immaterial nature of the essence there follows the immaterial nature of the power.

As to the thirteenth, it must be said that among accidents one is nearer than another to a subject; thus quantity is nearer to a substance than quality; and so a substance receives one accident by means of another; thus, for instance, it receives color by means of a surface, and knowledge by means of the intellectual power. In this way, then, a power of the soul is able to take on contraries, as a surface is able to take on white and black, inasmuch, namely, as the substance receives contraries in the way spoken of above.

As to the fourteenth, it must be said that the soul, insofar as it is the form of the body by its own essence, gives actual being to the body, inasmuch as it is a substantial form;[14] and it gives to it being of a certain sort, i.e., life, inasmuch as it is this kind of form, namely, a soul; and it gives it life of a certain sort, namely, in an intellectual nature, inasmuch as it is this kind of a soul, namely, intellectual. Now "understanding" sometimes means an activity, and in this sense its principle is a power or a habit; but sometimes it means precisely the actual being of an intellectual nature, and in this case the principle of understanding is the very essence of the intellectual soul.

As to the fifteenth, it must be said that the potency of matter is not a potency for acting, but for substantial being. And consequently the potency of matter can be in the genus "substance", but not the potency of the soul, which is a potency for acting.

As to the sixteenth, it must be said that, as was said above [ad 1], Augustine relates knowledge and love to the mind inasmuch as the mind is known and is loved; and if, because of this relationship, knowledge and love were in the mind or in the soul as in a subject, it would follow that by a parallel argument they would be in all things that are known and loved as in a subject: and in that case an accident would transcend its own subject, which is impossible. Otherwise, if Augustine were intending to prove that these were the very essence of the soul, his would be no proof. For it is no less true of the essence of a thing that

---

[14] These words "inasmuch as it is a substantial form" appear to be a gloss that was introduced into the text.

it does not exist outside the thing than it is true of an accident that it does not exist outside its subject.

As to the seventeenth, it must be said that from the very fast that the soul is free from matter by its own substance, it follows that it has an intellectual power, but not in such a way that its power is its own substance.

As to the eighteenth, it must be said that the intellect is not only an intellectual power, but much rather a substance because of its power; hence it is understood not only as a power but also as a substance.

As to the nineteenth, it must be said that the powers of the soul are called parts, not of the essence of the soul, but of its total power; just as if one were to say that the power of a bailiff is a part of the royal power as a whole.

As to the twentieth, it must be said that many of the powers of the soul are not in the soul as in a subject, but in the composite; and the multiformity of the parts of the body fits in with this multiplicity of powers. But the powers, which are in the substance of the soul alone as in a subject, are the agent intellect and the possible intellect, and the will. And for this multiplicity of powers it is sufficient that in the substance of the soul there is some composition of act and of potency, as was said above [Art. I].

MEDIAEVAL PHILOSOPHICAL TEXTS IN TRANSLATION

Translation #1: "Grosseteste: On Light"
by Clare Riedl-Trans.
This treatise is significant as an introduction to an influential thinker and man of science of the Middle Ages.

Translation #2: "St. Augustine: Against the Academicians"
by Sister Mary Patricia, R.S.M.-Trans.
Augustine aims to prove that man need not be content with mere probability in the realm of knowledge.

Translation #3: "Pico Della Mirandola: Of Being and Unity"
by Victor M. Hamm-Trans.
In this work Pico tried to discover the genuine thought of Plato and Aristotle on being and unity.

Translation #4: "Francis Suarez: On the Various Kinds of Distinction"
by Cyril Vollert, S.J.-Trans.
Suarez propounds his theory on distinctions, a point of capital importance for a grasp of Suarezian metaphysics.

Translation #5: "St. Thomas Aquinas: On Spiritual Creatures,"
by Mary C. Fitzpatrick-Trans.
This book falls into two general divisions: an introduction and the translation from the Latin.

Translation #6: "Meditations of Guigo,"
by John J. Jolin, S.J.-Trans.
A series of reflections by Guigo, 12th century Prior of the hermitage Charterhouse.

Translation #7: "Giles of Rome: Theorems on Existence and Essence,"
by Michael V. Murray, S.J.-Trans.
An essay dealing with the *a priori* deductions of being and its conditions.

Translation #8: "John of St. Thomas: Outlines of Formal Logic"
by Francis C. Wade, S.J.-Trans.
A standard English translation of the Logic of John of St. Thomas.

Translation #9: "Hugh of St. Victor: Soliloquy in the Earnest Money of the Soul,"
Kevin Herbert-Trans.
The purpose of the work is to direct the soul toward a true love of self, an attitude which is identical with a love of God.

Translation #10: "St. Thomas Aquinas: On Charity,"
by Lottie Kendzierski-Trans.
This treatise is significant as an expression of St. Thomas' discussion on the virtue of charity in itself, its object, subject, order, precepts, and principal act.

Translation #11: "Aristotle: On Interpretation-Commentary by St. Thomas and Cajetan,"
Jean T. Oesterle-Trans.
This translation will be of particular value to teachers and students of logic.

Translation #12: "Desiderius Erasmus of Rotterdam: On Copia of Words and Ideas,"
by Donald B. King and H. David Rix-Trans.
One of the most popular and influential books of the 16th century is made available here for the first time in English.

Translation #13: "Peter of Spain: Tractatus Syncategorematum and Selected Anonymous Treatises,"
by Joseph P. Mullally and Roland Houde-Trans.
The first English translation of these tracts now makes it possible for scholars of logic to better appreciate the continuity of Formal Logic.

Translation #14: "Cajetan: Commentary on St. Thomas Aquinas' On Being and Essence,"
by Lottie Kendzierski and Francis C. Wade, S.J.-Trans.
A basic understanding of the relation between Cajetan and St. Thomas.

Translation #15: "Suarez: Disputation VI, On Formal and Universal Unity,"
by James F. Ross-Trans.
The study of late mediaeval philosophy and the decline of scholasticism.

Translation #16: "St. Thomas, Sieger de Brabant, St. Bonaventure: On the Eternity of the World,"
by Cyril Vollert, S.J., Lottie Kendzierski, Paul Byrne-Trans.
A combined work bringing together the writings of three great scholars on the philosophical problem of the eternity of the world.

Translation #17: "Geoffrey of Vinsauf: Instruction in the Method and Art of Speaking and Versifying,"
by Roger P. Parr-Trans.
This text, of one of the most important mediaeval literary theorists, is here for the first time translated into English.

Translation #18: "Liber De Pomo: The Apple, or Aristotle's Death,"
by Mary F. Rousseau-Trans.
A significant item in the history of mediaeval thought, never previously translated into English from the Latin.

Translation #19: "St. Thomas Aquinas: On the Unity of the Intellect Against the Averroists,"
by Beatrice H. Zedler-Trans.
This is a polemical treatise that St. Thomas wrote to answer a difficult problem confronting his times.

Translation #20: "The Universal Treatise of Nicholas of Autrecourt,"
by Leonard L. Kennedy C.S.B., Richard E. Arnold, S.J. and Arthur E. Millward, A.M.
This treatise gives an indication of the deep philosophical skepticism at the University of Paris in the mid-fourteenth century.

Translation #21: "Pseudo-Dionysius Aeropagite: The Divine Names in Mystical Theology"
by John D. Jones-Trans.
Among the most important works in the transition from later Greek to Medieval thought.

Translation #22: "Matthew of Vendôme: Ars Versificatoria (The Art of the Versemaker)"
by Roger P. Parr-Trans.
The text of this, the earliest of the major treatises of the *Artes Poetical* is here translated in toto with special emphasis given to maintaining the full nature of the complete original text.